A three-masted ship ran ashore at Lowestoft in September 1909. In this picture, taken shortly before she broke up, boat guards can be seen in the rigging taking the sails down.

A Grim Almanac of
SUFFOLK

Neil R. Storey

Sutton Publishing Limited
Phoenix Mill · Thrupp · Stroud
Gloucestershire · GL5 2BU

First published 2004

Title page photograph: A skull on Dunwich beach.
Endpapers: A police funeral at Ipswich, *c.* 1910.

British Library Cataloguing in Publication Data
A catalogue record for this book is available from the British Library.

ISBN 0-7509-3498-0

Typeset in 10.5/13.5 Photina.
Typesetting and origination by
Sutton Publishing Limited.
Printed and bound in England by
J.H. Haynes & Co. Ltd, Sparkford.

This book is dedicated with gratitude to all those who have trod the beat in Suffolk over the years

(Suffolk Constabulary Archives)

CONTENTS

INTRODUCTION

Truth is always strange,
Stranger than fiction

Byron, *Don Juan* (1823)

Witness: He told me he had been reading books. The thought of robbing an old lady came upon him about a month before and he could not get rid of it.
His Lordship: Reading books on robberies I suppose?
Witness: Yes – 'penny dreadfuls'.

Exchange at the trial of a Lowestoft smacksman for murder,
Norfolk & Suffolk Assizes, 1905

In the early nineteenth century a strange phenomenon began to manifest itself and become evident throughout all strata of British society; its roots were ancient and to be found in the earliest recorded stories – a fascination with 'ghoulies, ghosties and long-leggedy beasties'. Everyone enjoys the thrill and chill of a good horror story but it is always that little more piquant if there is an edge of truth to the tale and it relates to a past incident or occurrence in the same locality. One of the earliest recorded British poltergeist phenomena was noted during the reign of Richard I (1151–99) at the home of Sir Osborne of Bradwell at Dagworth in Suffolk. This spirit spoke to a number of people, revealing 'the secret doings of others'.

Britain in the nineteenth century was a very different country from now. Death was far more of a feature of everyday life. Families were large; parents knew few of their children would reach adulthood. In the mid-nineteenth century, with its epidemic diseases, squalid living conditions, poor sanitation and dangerous machinery and industrial processes, the average life expectancy of a country labourer was about 38 years, while in cities of the industrial north a man could expect to live, on average, until about the age of 17.

There was a strong feeling, especially among the poorer classes, that even though they were on the poverty line they would give their beloved family members 'a good send off'. Even on some of the poorest streets, the clatter of a horse-drawn hearse would be familiar, complete with black horses in harness and plumes, and attended by coffin-bearers in top hats with long black crêpe 'weepers'. If this was not enough, a further carriage could be supplied for family mourners and extras such as feathermen in great canopies of plumes, and mute mourners could be hired. Social commentator Mrs Bernard Bosanquet, in her 1899 book *Rich and Poor*, observed, 'The greatest festival of all is perhaps the funeral . . . the poverty of the family makes no difference to their eagerness . . . I have known a woman have a hearse and four horses, and a carriage and pair, for her husband's funeral, and within two weeks apply to the Guardians to feed her children.'

For many, a Sunday constitutional would consist of a visit to the local cemetery to tend the graves of deceased family and friends. This activity led to many good people casting their eyes over other headstones and realising some might be those of the famous, bear unusual carvings or record curious prose or deaths; very soon ladies and gentlemen began collecting epitaphs from gravestones much in the way butterfly or bird-egg collectors sought out their quarry. Even at fairs and public entertainment, death and horror were on display. Most travelling fairs would include a freak show which, beside the living human curiosities, would have dead ones displayed in jars of alcohol. Even on the beaches of Suffolk, especially around Orford Ness, a boy would be quite disappointed if he could not find a skull on the beach to show (or frighten) mother. Such grim relics were washed up after the churchyards of Dunwich gradually crumbled into the sea. This was a time when prisons and bridewells were still in evidence in the county towns. Most people would walk past gaols and see hands at the bars, hear the noise and inhale the smell of the prisons and prisoners as a matter of course and think nothing of it – it was simply a feature of everyday life.

As more and more people became literate and newspapers, books and periodicals became widely available and affordable, it was not long before authors were inspired to create their own stories of ghosts, horror, death and suspense. The first within this genre was Mary Shelley's classic *Frankenstein*, published in 1818. Throughout the nineteenth century such horror stories were supplemented by 'penny dreadfuls' such as *Sweeney Todd the Demon Barber of Fleet Street*, *Spring Heel'd Jack* and *Varney the Vampire*, finally reaching their zenith on the blood-soaked pages of Bram Stoker's *Dracula* in 1897. Judiciary and public were quick to condemn these books as a bad influence on the lower classes but most could not resist a peek. This was the hypocrisy of society at the time. Authorities for the most part ignored vile practices like backstreet abortions and baby-farming, while many read every last lurid detail of the latest suicide, accident or murder recorded in the newspaper.

Until 1869, when some saw the barbarity of this act and ordered that it be conducted behind prison doors, one of *the* most popular and well-attended public occasions was the public execution. After following the case from the 'discovery of the horror', through reported interviews with witnesses, their friends and neighbours, apprehension, and trial in the newspapers, onlookers would have amassed, having exchanged views in pubs and meeting-places, some sympathy or hatred for the accused – and the denouement of it all would be the public execution. Literally thousands would gather from the early hours of the morning in front of the county gaols at Ipswich and Bury St Edmunds where a raised platform or stage with gallows-beam allowed all to

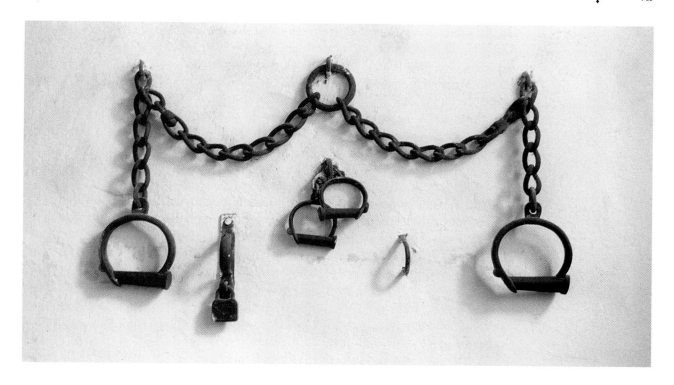

Leg irons and handcuffs from the old lock-up at Wenhaston Church.

see. The 'event' was similar in mood to that of a sporting occasion today. Among the crowd would be hot pie-and-potato sellers; beer and gin would flow; even hot nuts were sold in the winter time. Above the hubbub would be the stentorian voices of the long song or broadsheet sellers who would, for about a ha'penny, sell a sheet with a suitable engraving (the condemned man on the gallows, the murder, or the criminal in his cell, etc.) which would outline the facts of the case, record the 'final confession', and might even contain a selection of verse on the dastardly deed. Crime and horror was to the Victorians what 'The Grand Tour' had been to the Georgians – there was a roaring trade in souvenirs and stiff competition for the prime purpose of enhancing a cabinet of curiosities. A small payment to a gaoler or hangman could secure a button, letter, a lock of hair, or even a section of the actual rope. After the execution of William Corder, the notorious Red Barn Murderer, the rope was sold by executioner Foxton at a guinea an inch.

Once the spectacle of public hanging was stopped, the curiosity did not abate, and so arose the first of the gutter press – *The Illustrated Police News* – one of the most widely circulated periodicals of the latter half of the nineteenth century. This paper was profusely illustrated with graphic depictions of crimes in progress, 'based on witness statements', victims (before and after death), the detectives and policemen involved, as well as sketches of crime scenes and suspects which led to many a suspicious eye and fist being thrown at perfectly innocent people. With executions conducted behind closed doors, reporters were allowed to observe in the hanging chamber but this practice was discontinued by 1910. After this time reporters still tried to give the impression of some 'inside knowledge' of the procedure of execution. Methods of execution developed apace between 1910 and the abolition of hanging in Britain in 1964. Still, the reporters insisted on detailing long-obsolete procedures such as the walk to the execution chamber led by the priest reading the 23rd Psalm and the boom of the falling gallows trap sounding throughout the prison. Only with the publication of memoirs by the likes of Public Executioner Albert Pierrepoint after abolition were many of the old 'myths' finally dispensed with. By the time of abolition most prisons had condemned cells with adjoining hanging chambers, and an execution – from entering the cell to the drop of the trap and dislocation of vertebrae – would normally be completed in the time it took the prison clock to strike 8 o'clock – a maximum of about 25 seconds.

But what of dear old Suffolk, the beautiful rural county of mellow colours, wide open skies, and rural charm recorded by its great artist sons Gainsborough and Constable – could it really yield enough grim stories for a book? My first clue came from an old rhyme which appears in several forms, each seeming to change the place names to suit the bias of the writer. One version is as follows:

> Beccles for a Puritan, Bungay for the poor,
> Halesworth for a drunkard and Bliburgh for a whore.
> Ipswich for water dogs, Southwold for pluck,
> Begger old Lowstuff, how black she do look.

Arthur Mee said of the county in his *King's England* guide of 1941, 'Suffolk is a county a little apart'. He meant this in the sense that it was the farthest east in England and that it was ostensibly an unspoilt rural county. In a grim almanac this can also be seen as referring to a county a little different, a little apart from the mainstream, where folklore lasted a little longer and the belief in the paranormal was a little stronger.

It did not take much research to discover England's last major witch trial was held at Bury St Edmunds in 1664. This was after a reign of terror in which Witchfinder General Matthew Hopkins examined over 200 people in Suffolk for witchcraft. After enduring horrific tests, from pricking and swimming to sleep deprivation, about sixty-eight people were 'proved witches' and sent to their doom in Suffolk alone during 1645 and 1646. With a little further investigation, evidence of generations of witches may be found in Suffolk. One of the earliest named and recorded witches was Margery Jourdemayne, the famous witch of Eye, who was patronised by the Duchess of Gloucester during the reign of Henry VI (1421–71). In Margery's footsteps followed 'Owd Nan Barret' who enjoyed a great reputation throughout Norfolk and Suffolk for forty years. One would think that, after the hideous blood-letting of the Hopkins years, the witch fear would be truly quenched – not so in Suffolk! In 1693 Samuels Petts, 'Minister of the Gospel at Sudbury', published a thirty-five-page pamphlet on the bewitchment of Thomas Spatchett (late of Dunwich and Cookley). Even into the late eighteenth

Lowestoft Cemetery.

century poor souls were still being swum and accused of witchcraft in Suffolk. The last recorded swimming in Suffolk was of a supposed wizard at Wickham Skeith in July 1825.

Once one scratches the surface of any county's history there is soon some old pus and corruption to be squeezed out; Suffolk is by no means an exception. Consider the literary doyens of the county: M.R. James, arguably the creator of the modern ghost story, spent most of his childhood at Livermere Rectory where, although he was quite happy, his dreams were plagued by many a nightmare. When George Orwell (later famous for his sinister vision of the future in *1984*) was staying at Southwold in July 1931 he took a stroll to Walberswick Church. While sitting nearby and enjoying the view, Orwell noticed 'a small and stooping man' dressed in brown enter

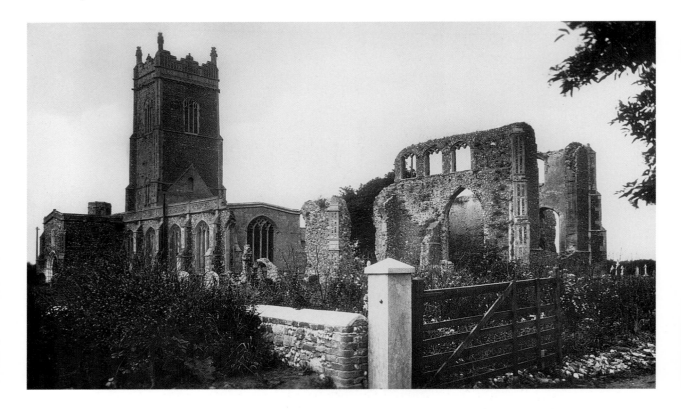

Walberswick Church,
c. 1910.

the churchyard. Struck with the realisation that the man had made no noise, Orwell followed the path taken by the figure to find he had disappeared! Even modern murder-mystery writers such as P.D. James and Ruth Rendell have property in the county and use locations in Suffolk as settings and inspiration for their tales.

Wild men, devil dogs, green children and even a werewolf make up the core of the oldest folk tales of Suffolk. Such tales are complimented by many grim relics across the county such as wayside suicide graves, unusual tombstones, disembodied heads, a book bound in the skin of a murderer, and even the heart of a queen of England, but many more tales are now crammed into this volume from burnings of heretics and once-notorious crimes, criminals and their punishment, to freaks, strange deaths and disasters, all jostling for position in this cornucopia of the macabre. This book has been made possible by generations of collectors, historians, authors and reporters who included strange stories and detailed gory accounts in their publications. I have simply noted them down and followed their leads, planning to do something one day with the file marked 'Strange Suffolk'. Combining these stories with generous and privileged access to coroners' reports, inquest accounts, assize records, private collections, public libraries and police archives, I have plumbed the depths of many of the dustiest and longest-forgotten records of the past. In an unashamed investigation into the not-so-good-old-days, join me on a journey along the darker paths of Suffolk's history – enter . . . if you dare!

Neil R. Storey, 2004

January

Lowestoft police station, policemen and cells matron, *c.* 1880.
(Suffolk Police Archives)

1 JANUARY   **1721**   Edwin Crispe was attacked by John Woodburn, armed with a billhook, while Crispe was walking to a coffee-house after an evening function with his brother-in-law, Arundel Coke. Coke was not expecting to see his friend Edwin ever again! But lo, a hideous vision walked into the festivities; throat cut, both cheeks cut and nose split in two, horribly injured but very much alive, it was Edwin Crispe! The news of the terrible deed soon spread across the town and local blacksmith John Carter could hold his tongue no more; he had been approached to assassinate Crispe. It transpired that Coke's sister stood to inherit Crispe's money if the latter died (his children all having died previously, possibly poisoned by Coke). When Woodburn had abortively attempted the killing of Crispe, Coke had offered the well-paid but dastardly job to Carter, who turned it down flat. After temporary loss of speech, Crispe recovered his voice and revealed what he knew: Coke and Woodburn were soon on trial. Found guilty, both were executed on 31 March 1721; Coke, paid for a quiet execution at 6 a.m. while Woodburn went to his death in front of a huge crowd on Tayfen Meadows.

2 JANUARY   **1868**   Seventeen-year-old William Beer was given fourteen days' hard labour, having been found by a patrolling constable to be playing dice in Sudbury market place.

3 JANUARY   **1899**   Two boys playing in Christchurch Park, Ipswich, heard the report of a pistol on the east side of the Wilderness Pond. Running to the spot near the rails bordering the avenue, they saw a man lying flat on his back with his head against a tree. Mr T. Damant, the park-keeper, and one of his assistants named Battram examined the body which Mr Damant recognised as a regular visitor and leading light of Nonconformism, Mr W.H. Bond. A closer examination

Christchurch
Mansion, *c.* 1900.

revealed his hat was off and a revolver was in his right hand. Bond had shot himself in the right temple, but the bullet had failed to exit the other side of his head and, although unconscious, he was still alive. Dr Moseley was sent for and ordered Bond's immediate removal to the Ipswich and East Suffolk Hospital. Bond died three hours later. At the inquest a verdict of suicide while of unsound mind was delivered.

4 JANUARY

1907 East Suffolk Quarter Sessions heard the case of William Goshawk, 'an incorrigible'. Goshawk (36) had been convicted at Stowmarket Magistrates' Court for destroying a door and glass, valued £5 5s, the property of the Guardians of Stow Union (another name for the workhouse) and as he had been previously convicted several times, he was sent to the Sessions to be dealt with as 'an incorrigible rogue'. The prisoner, when asked to make a statement, said: 'Well it's like this. To see the task of work in the union, I would rather be in prison, for the food is better there than it is in the workhouse.' The chairman said he was 'not disposed to accede to the prisoner's request and make his life too pleasant', and handed him five calendar months' imprisonment.

5 JANUARY

1847 Rose Ann Sare, a little girl of nine, was picking up coprolites on Bawdsey Beach with some friends. This innocent occupation earned the children a shilling a bushel from a local tradesman, who turned these fossilised phosphates into fertiliser. During their searches Rose went closer to the cliffs than the others and, fatefully, when all their eyes were concentrating on the ground, part of the cliff swiftly and without warning fell onto the beach burying young Rose. Her distressed friends ran for help but by the time her father and three other men had arrived to dig her out, she was tragically beyond help.

6 JANUARY

1427 On or about this date the body of Thomas Beaufort, Duke of Exeter, son of John of Gaunt, leader of the English rearguard at the Battle of Agincourt and Defender of Harfleur, was brought to the Abbey church of Bury St Edmunds and laid near the body of his Duchess in the Chapel of Our Lady. In 1772 his body was uncovered in its lead coffin by some labourers breaking up part of the ruins of the church. Before it was realised who they had disinterred, the coffin was opened to reveal 'an embalmed body, as fresh and entire as at time of interment, surrounded by a kind of pickle and the face covered with a clerecloth. The features, the nails of the fingers and toes, and the hair, which was brown with some mixture of grey, appeared as perfect as ever'. A surgeon, hearing of the discovery, went to examine the body. Following an incision in the breast 'the flesh cut as firm as that of a living subject and there was even an appearance of blood'. The skull was sawn in pieces to examine the brain. Note was made that at the time it did not smell offensive but with exposure to air 'soon became putrid'. The labourers, for the sake of the lead, removed the body from its coffin and threw it on the rubbish. This terrible abuse of the noble Thomas Beaufort was detected just in time, and his remains were rescued and reburied in a strong oak coffin at the foot of the north-east pillar which once supported the Abbey belfry.

7 JANUARY   **1646**   A sum of £2 was paid to Matthew Hopkins, Witchfinder General, by the Chamberlain of Aldeburgh for giving evidence against witches in the gaol. Hopkins and a certain Goody Phillips had already been paid £2 and £1 respectively for 'finding out witches' in the town the previous September; they had repeated this process in December. The account book concludes: 'Paid six men to ward at the sessions and execution for two days and a half at 12*d* per day, and 6*d* to drink . . . Paid John Pame, eleven shillings for hanging seven witches. Paid Mr Dannell, £1 for the gallows, and setting them up. For a post to set by the grave of the dead bodies that were hanged and for burying of them, six shillings. Paid Henry Lawrence the Roper, eight shillings for seven halter and making the knots.'

The Ancient Moot Hall at Aldeburgh, *c.* 1905.

1933   Police from Glemsford were summoned by Betsy Elliott to the small gypsy encampment near the railway station where her husband, Everitt, had been shot and killed. When she arrived with the police officer, Robert Munday – the man who fired the fatal shot – was just returning from the police station at Foxearth where he had turned himself in. Then the sturdy policeman's reply had been to instruct Munday to return to the scene of the crime and await the policeman, who soon arrived on his bike. Arrest was swift and the whole sordid story emerged at the assizes in February. After a night of drinking and minor altercations, an exchange had occurred when those involved had returned to their ramshackle dwellings. In the heat of an argument, Munday fetched his shotgun, intending to frighten Elliot. Instead, as he raised the old gun it went off, loosing the one good barrel it had at close range to Elliot, blowing off the left hand side of his face and skull. The defence was eloquent; the witness's statements were robust and convincing. Judge and jury were satisfied Munday did not act with intent and he was acquitted.

1888   George Thurgood of Wickhambrook was brought before Haverhill Petty Sessions for searching for work in clothes that were the property of the workhouse. Despite his insistence that he was just looking for gainful employment, Thurgood was sentenced to fourteen days' hard labour.

1762   Mary, the daughter of John Weatherset, alias Downing, aged 16, was taken ill with pains in her left leg, then her foot and toes. Next day her whole foot had swollen and black spots appeared on her toes. By the time the blackening reached her knee the flesh of her leg had putrefied and come off at the ankle, leaving the leg bones bare. Despite attendance by local surgeons, by April, Mary's mother, father, sister Elizabeth (14) and brothers Robert (7) and Edward (4) had all had their feet simply rot off. Even the mother's newborn child was seized with the disorder and died. A mural tablet records the events of 1762 but no one was ever able to say what caused 'The Wattisham Affliction'.

1845   Mary Shemming (51) of Martlesham was executed at the County Gaol, Ipswich for murder.

1905   Charles Hoy Fort (1874–1932), the father of modern phenomenalism and Fortean research, collected a vast library of books and cuttings relating to the bizarre, unusual and unexplained. An article from the *East Anglian Daily Times* on this day firmly entered his collection. The report described a mysterious man who appeared in the county carrying a book with writings and drawings in an unknown language; the man even spoke in the same strange tongue.

1827   George Southgate was incarcerated in Ipswich Gaol to await transportation to the penal colonies for seven years after being found guilty of stealing flour. He was far from unique. Between 1787 and 1868 thousands of male and female British criminals (some under 10 years of age) were transported in prison hulks to Australia. Their crimes varied from three instances of petty theft to rioting. Locked in irons and in dock for months before departure on the 252-day journey, most were already weak and malnourished. As many as a quarter of the passengers would die before they reached Botany Bay.

14 JANUARY   **1328**   On this night a tempest hit the coast of Suffolk and began the decline of the prosperous fishing port of Dunwich. The hurricane winds drove the sea against the spit of land known as the King's Holme and pushed it into the harbour area, effectively rendering it impassable. All trade and revenues simply moved to Walberswick and left Dunwich to rot. Four hundred houses along with shops, barns, windmills and two churches, St Martin and St Leonard, fell in the maelstrom. All of the other churches and chapels gradually fell into the sea, with most of the town gone by the early years of the twentieth century. Despite the decline it still maintained the ancient right to return two Members of Parliament. By the time of the 1832 Reform Act, which abolished rotten boroughs like Dunwich, there were only eight residents left in the constituency!

15 JANUARY   **1327**   There was a great riot at Bury, where the town gates were broken down and the abbey was raided. The monks carried out an armed reprisal raid on townsfolk when at worship, and thirty cartloads of prisoners ended up being dispatched to Norwich to face trial.

The ruins of All Saints' Church, Dunwich, *c.* 1905. No trace of this church or the cliffs where it stood remains today.

1881 There was a report of John Brown, the escaped convict, being brought to Ipswich Gaol. Brown had been sentenced to three months' hard labour the previous October at Bury Quarter Sessions. Removed from the dock, Brown was then escorted to Bury railway station. After going to use the toilet facilities there he found both warders had their backs to the exit and they were enjoying a good laugh as if Brown was not there. As the judge commented at the hearing after his recapture, 'You saw they did not care about you and you did not care about imprisonment. I can see that there is very good reason to suppose that there was a great temptation for you.' In view of these circumstances, the amount of time Brown had already served while waiting for court appearances and the non-violence in his recapture, the judge saw fit to be lenient and sentenced him to seven days' hard labour.

THE

Town and Borough of Ipswich,

Suffolk to Wit.

A CALENDAR of the PRISONERS in the Custody of R. FLETCHER, for Trial at the General Quarter Sessions of the Peace, and General Gaol Delivery, to be holden at the Old Shire Hall, in and for the said Town and Borough, and the Liberties thereof, before

SIR CHARLES FREDERICK WILLIAMS, KNT.

Recorder of the said Town and Borough, on Thursday, the Seventh Day of January, 1841.

CHARLOTTE PAYNE, aged 17 — Committed 23rd November, 1840, by James Ram, Esq., and others, charged on the oaths of Maria Chamberlain and another, with having stolen one Neckerchief and other articles, the property of Robert Chamberlain.
(R).

2 JAMES THOMAS WEST, aged 50 — Committed 11th November, 1840, by John Ridley, Esqr., charged on the oaths of William Henry Sheldrake and others, with having stolen one pair of Woman's Boots, the property of the said William Henry Sheldrake.
(R. W. Well.)

3 The said JAMES THOMAS WEST, — Stands further charged on the oaths of Thomas Hambly and others, with having stolen Eight Brass Taps, the Property of William Singleton.

4 The said JAMES THOMAS WEST, — Also stands charged on the oaths of Mary Pilch and another, with having stolen one Brass Candlestick and one Brass Pestle, the property of the said Mary Pilch.

5 The said JAMES THOMAS WEST, — Also stands charged on the oaths of Rosamond Ungless and others, with having stolen one Copper Gallon Can, the property of the said Rosamond Ungless.

6 ROBERT KING, aged 18 — Committed 26th December, 1840, by John Ridley, Esq., charged on the oaths of John Limmer and others, with having stolen Two Pounds weight of Currants and other articles, the property of the said John Limmer.
(R)

7 WILLIAM WILLIAMS, aged 11 — Committed 19th November, 1840, by James Ram, Esq., and others, charged on the oaths of Richard Mayston and another, with having stolen Three Sixpences, the monies of the said Richard Mayston.
(R).
discharged on Bail 30th November.

8 GEORGE ANKIN, aged 17 — Committed 30th October, 1840, by Benjamin Brame, Esq., and another, charged on the oaths of Simon Girling and another, with having stolen Four Pecks and a Half of Wheat, and other Wheat, the property of Thomas Prentice, Hammond Kemball, and Robert Squirrell.
(R.)

9 JOHN JOHNSON, aged 25 — Committed 11th December, 1840, by Benjamin Brame, Esq., and others, charged on the oaths of John Hillyard and another, with having obtained a Stuff Waistcoat, the property of the said John Hillyard, by a false pretence.
(R. W. Imp.)

10 DAVID MANNING, aged 23 — Committed 17th December, 1840, by Peter Bw. Long, Esq., and others, charged on the oaths of George Higgitt and others, with having stolen one Six-pence and Three-pence half-penny, the monies of the said George Higgitt, from the person of the said George Higgitt.
(R. W. Imp.)

11 WILLIAM WILLETT, aged 25 . — Committed 30th November, 1840, by Peter Bw. Long, Esq., and others, charged on the oaths of Michael Ryan and others, the said James Burrows and William Snell, with having stolen one Truss, containing Six Damask Table Cloths, and divers other goods, the property of the said Michael Ryan, and the said William Willett, with having received the said goods, knowing the same to have been stolen.
(R)
JAMES BURROWS, aged 24
(R)
WILLIAM SNELL, aged 21
(R. W. Imp.)

12 The said WILLIAM WILLETT, — Stands further charged on the oaths of William Scotford and others, with having stolen Six-Hundred and a Half of Quills and other goods, the property of the said William Scotford.

13 The said WILLIAM WILLETT, — Stands further charged on the oaths of John Thomas Messer and others, with having stolen one Shirt, one Shirt Front, and other apparel, the property of the said John Thomas Messer.

14 WILLIAM BRETT, aged 32 — Committed 1st December, 1840, by Peter Bw. Long, Esq. and another charged on the oaths of William Bayley and others, on suspicion of having stolen one Peck and an Half of Beans, the property of Thomas Prentice, Hammond Kemball, and Robert Squirrell.
(R. W. Imp.)
discharged on Bail 3rd December.

15 JOSEPH HARVEY, aged 17 — Committed 21st December, 1840, by Peter Bw. Long, Esq., charged on the oaths of Margaret Woollard and others, with having burglariously broken and entered the Dwelling-House of William Woollard, and stolen therefrom Fifteen Shillings in Silver, and Five Shillings in Copper Coin, the monies of the said William Woollard.
(R)
WILLIAM READ, aged 20
(R. W. Imp.)

(Suffolk Police Archives)

17 JANUARY **1888** The Rector of Pakefield publicly defended his stance in criticising the Mayor of Lowestoft for holding a New Year ball, on the grounds that dancing for entertainment was evil. Opening his statement the rector quoted St John Chrysostom: 'For where there is dancing there is the devil.' He then spelt out his six points of disapproval which included: 'Men were deemed infamous who perverted dancing from a sacred use to amusement'; 'No instances occur of the two sexes uniting in the exercise of social dancing for amusement'; and 'there is no instance of social dancing except that of the vain fellows devoid of shame . . . and of Herodians which led to the murder of John the Baptist'. The editor of the *Argus* went on record, in response to the Rector, stating, 'He would have made an admirable sergeant in Cromwell's bodyguard of psalm-smiters but he is less adapted to the care of souls pertaining to more latter day bodies.' I wonder if the rector had ever heard the rhyme:

Below: Postcard sold to help endow the Porters' Cot Scheme for Children in the East Suffolk & Ipswich Hospital, *c.* 1910.

The roaring boys of Pakefield,
Oh, how they all do thrive!
They had but one poor parson
And him they buried alive.

EAST SUFFOLK & IPSWICH HOSPITAL

Verily I say unto you inasmuch as ye have done it unto one of the least of these my little sick ones ye have done it unto me.

J. MOSS, Head Porter.

SCHEME TO ENDOW COT. COST £500.

County Bridewells and Gaols visited by Prison Reformer John Howard 18 JANUARY
Howard visited Woodbridge Bridewell in 1776, 1779 and 1782; his observations here were uncharacteristically clipped: 'Two rooms, lately enlarged, 28ft by 16ft: in these are beds and bedding: the lower one is 9ft high. To each are three windows and a fireplace. The court is also enlarged out of the keeper's garden and made secure.' Howard notes the keepers' salary at £15 and concludes: 'Prisoners allowance, two pence per day. No firing: no water: no employment (to occupy the prisoners).'

1944 US courts martial of Leatherberry and Fowler were held at Ipswich 19 JANUARY
Town Hall. Their crime was committed on 8 December 1943 between Colchester and Marney. Their plan was a get-rich-quick scheme to rob a taxi driver at some lonely spot and run away into the darkness. They picked up a taxi driven by Harry Hailstone and before they had a chance to move their plan into action, Fowler asked the driver to pull over because he was desperate to urinate. Returning from the roadside after relieving himself, he saw Leatherberry and the taxi driver in a desperate struggle in which Leatherberry succeeded in strangling Harry Hailstone to death. The pair set about concealing the body by pushing it under a wire fence from whence they watched it roll down a slope. They then drove off in the taxi, dumping it at Layer Marney. After some keen detective work Fowler and Leatherberry were traced. Evidence such as bloodstained clothes recovered from Leatherberry's locker and the evidence of his accomplice, Fowler, saw them stand trial at Ipswich Town Hall where, because they were military personnel, they faced the courts martial. Both were found guilty. Fowler received a life sentence while Leatherberry had sentence of death passed on him. Execution of US serviceman J.C. Leatherberry was carried out on 16 March 1944 at Shepton Mallet prison, Somerset.

1909 George Arthur Wilkinson (27), a stableman of Bury St Edmunds, stood 20 JANUARY
trial at the Suffolk Assizes for the murder of Evelyn Adeline Buddle at Bury St Edmunds on 17 October 1908. Wilkinson was 'keeping company' with Blanche Buddle (18) who had already had a child by him. Blanche and her daughter lived on Mainwater Lane with her father and two sisters, May Elizabeth (15) and 'Eva' Evelyn (8). On the night of 16 October, Wilkinson called round, took Blanche out drinking and stayed on the couch until the morning. Going out for a while, he returned at about 10 a.m. At that time Blanche and Eva were upstairs and May downstairs. Wilkinson gave the latter child a halfpenny and told her to go to buy some chocolates. He then called for Eva to come downstairs and struck her with at least four violent blows on the head with the poker from the back kitchen; he then rushed upstairs and attempted to attack Blanche with it. He was not serious in his attack, and she soon wrested the poker from him and ran downstairs. May came home and Wilkinson said, 'Be quiet, I am going to give myself up', and sure enough Wilkinson arrived at the police station and did just that. The poor little girl Eva was removed to hospital and died a few hours later, her skull badly

fractured. At the trial the mental state of Wilkinson was brought into question and the medical evidence was so compelling that the jury agreed Wilkinson could not have been responsible for his actions and was duly sentenced 'to be kept in custody until His Majesty's pleasure was known'.

21 JANUARY   **1880**   *Money for old rope.* The case was heard at Lowestoft police court of Thomas Garwood (39) who pleaded guilty to having stolen 14st of old rope and 2st of salt beef to the value of 27s from the schooner, *Albion*, the property of John Grindell. Garwood had sold the rope to Samuel Bagshaw, a marine store dealer, for 12s. The prisoner received two months' imprisonment with hard labour.

22 JANUARY   **1905**   Details were published and circulated following the arrival of the smack *Integrity* at Lowestoft and the reported loss of Thomas Spall, one of the crew. A single man from Lowestoft, Spall was last seen when the smack was about 70 miles south-east of the port. The sea was calm. Spall had been seen on deck, alone, plaiting a rope but later he was missing and the handspike he had been using was gone. It was surmised that when the vessel rolled he was jerked overboard.

Fishing smacks set sail from Lowestoft Harbour, *c.* 1905.

Strange and Horrible Tales of Suffolk

Dick Turpin, the notorious highwayman.

Sometime in the winter of 1739 the notorious highwayman Dick Turpin and his partner in crime, Tom King, started from London and took a ride to Bungay. In the town they espied two young ladies receive £14 for corn and Turpin resolved to relieve them of it. King remonstrated with the old scallywag by saying 'it was a pity to take the money from such pretty girls'. But the horrible, pock-marked little man that was the real Dick Turpin persisted and took the girls for all they had. Turpin eventually ended up killing his friend Tom King by mistake while trying to evade capture, but captured he was, and executed at York as a highwayman, horse-stealer and murderer on 10 April 1739.

Suffolk beliefs and omens that warn of the approach of the Angel of Death

If a corpse is supple after death, it is a sign that there will be another death in that family before very long.

———•—•———

During the interval between death and burial a body is spoken of as 'lying by the wall'. An old saying in the county states: 'If one lie by the wall on Sunday there will be another [another corpse in the same parish] before the week is out'.

———•—•———

If a grave is open on a Sunday, there will be another dug before the week is out.

1845   William Howell (28) was executed for murder at Ipswich Gaol. Three local 'characters known to the police' – namely William Howell, his brother Walter (21) and Israel Shipley (38), while breaking into a barn at Gisleham, were disturbed by village constable James McFadden.

In the act of confronting the men, the constable had a shotgun levelled at him by Will Howell and was warned off. Bravely continuing to effect the arrest of the three, Constable McFadden carried on his approach unperturbed. Will blasted a shot from his gun, inflicting a serious wound to McFadden's thigh and causing him to collapse in agony to the floor where Walter Howell and Shipley set about kicking him and then ran off.

Constable McFadden managed to drag himself to a nearby farmhouse where he recounted the incident and named his assailants. Conveyed to his home in Kessingland and given what medical treatment was at hand, sadly the brave constable succumbed to his wounds. The three criminals were soon rounded up and sent to trial, where all three were found guilty of murder and sentenced to death. Walter Howell and Israel Shipley's sentences were commuted to transportation for life to Norfolk Island while Will Howell suffered the full force of the law and was executed in front of a massive crowd at Ipswich Gaol.

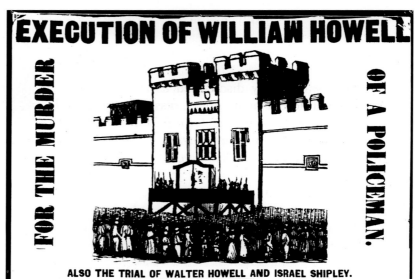

(Suffolk Police Archives)

1885   The 'Tichbourne Claimant' appeared with Sanger's Circus at Ipswich. *26 JANUARY*
The Tichbourne trial was for many years Britain's longest and a national
sensation in its day. Arthur Orton, a 27st Wapping-born butcher, had
answered one of the appeals published in papers all over the world by
Lady Tichbourne in her desperate search for her missing son, Sir
Roger. The emotional and frantic Lady Tichbourne was totally taken
in by the subterfuge of Orton, who posed as her long-lost son. Others
were not going to be so easily duped, especially as they could see
this rogue inheriting a considerable fortune. Lady Tichbourne
died before the case came to trial but therein over the weeks
and months Orton was totally discredited as the heir by his
want of public school accent or manners, dissimilarity in build
and lack of tattoo on the forearm known to have featured on the
real Sir Roger. The trial lasted 1,025 days and the jury took just
thirty minutes to find Orton guilty of imposture; a sentence of fourteen
years with hard labour was meted out. After his release Orton joined Sanger's
Circus and travelled the country as a curiosity telling of his life and adventures.

Arthur Orton, the
'Tichborne Claimant'.

1893   *Reported case of drowning in the baptistry of Botesdale Gospel Hall.* Mrs *27 JANUARY*
Elizabeth Garnham, a woman who lived near the chapel, took in washing and
was allowed to use the rainwater collected in the chapel's tank. She was
assisted in her labours by Mrs Larter who was passing the chapel and noticed
the doors were open. Entering to investigate, she noticed Mrs Garnham's
slippers and shawl on the floor, and Mrs Garnham quite dead and floating in
the tank. The inquest heard Mrs Garnham was 'down in her spirits' and had
previously suffered with 'inflammation of the brain'. A verdict of 'suicide
while temporarily insane' was recorded.

1787   The following was published in the *Ipswich Journal* without any remark *28 JANUARY*
of its being an unusual occurrence: 'A farmer of the parish of Stowupland sold
his wife to a neighbour for five guineas, and being happy to think he had made
a good bargain, presented her with a guinea to buy her a new gown; he then
went to Stowmarket, and gave orders for the bells to be rung upon the occasion.'

Suffolk Old Dame's Leechcraft
29 JANUARY

Cures for whooping cough
Procure a live flat fish, a 'little dab' will do; place it whilst alive on the bare
chest of the patient, and keep it there until the fish is dead.

If several children are ailing, take some of the hair of the eldest child, cut it
into small pieces, and put them into some milk and give the compound to the
youngest child to drink, and so on through the family.

Let the patient eat a mouse or let the patient
drink some milk that a ferret has lapped or let the
patient be dragged under a gooseberry bush or
bramble, both ends of which are growing in the
ground.

30 JANUARY

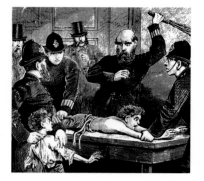

1880   The case was reported of Thomas Waller, a boy aged eleven, who appeared at court in Ipswich. Apparently the lad had observed a postman putting letters in a tradesman's box. Pushing his slender arm and small hands through the letter-box he extracted one of the letters. Opening it he discovered a cheque for £82 and suggested to one of his pals that they go to London on a spending spree. His pal did not like the idea and, his conscience pricked, the boy confessed all to his mother. Justice was, however, seen to be done and described in court as 'a proper subject for the birch', Waller received six strokes and served three days' imprisonment.

31 JANUARY

Charles Drew junior shoots his father on his doorstep.
(Johnson Collection)

1740   In one of the most notorious cases to rock the county of Suffolk in the eighteenth century, it emerged that the rich and spoilt upbringing of young Charles Drew junior saw him indulge in a world of prostitutes, coffee-houses, high living and drink. As his money ran low he borrowed from friends and became involved in smuggling. Charles Drew senior was quite fed up with his son's irresponsible behaviour, and it was the final straw when he heard the young man had put the house-keeper of Liston Hall in the family way: he cut off his allowance but fatally he did not cut the boy out of his will. Enlisting the help of Edward Humphries, Drew junior sought in vain for an assassin and so borrowed a gun from Liston Hall and returned as the potential killer of his father and inheritor of his wealth. On this chilly morning at about 6 a.m. the body of poor old Charles Drew senior was found thrice shot on his doorstep on Hall Street, Long Melford. Humphries was accused of the murder and slammed into Bury Gaol. A letter was smuggled out to Drew, pleading for help, but was delivered in error to one Timothy Drew. The game was up and constables were soon detailed to trace Charles Drew junior. He was arrested in London, detained at Newgate and brought in irons and with a heavy escort to Bury to stand trial in March 1740. Humphries saved his skin by turning King's evidence and ensured Drew kept his appointment with the hangman.

FEBRUARY

Dr Rowland Taylor rebukes a 'Popish Priest' about to say Mass in his church at Hadleigh.
Dr Taylor was ultimately martyred for his beliefs on 8 February 1555.

1 FEBRUARY **1921** Two Londoners, Arthur James Parsley (19) and Frank Jarvis (18), entered the Beccles branch of Lloyds Bank armed with revolvers and demanded the cashier hand over the money. The pair made their escape with a wad of notes. Beccles police were swiftly notified and Inspector Norman lost no time organising a search and a force-wide circulation of their descriptions. Intelligence soon returned that two men matching the robbers' descriptions had left on the Lowestoft train. Further information came in that men answering their descriptions had had lunch at the Horse Shoes pub at North Cove and had been subsequently spotted in Worlingham. Inspector Norman knew he needed transport so he called on local auctioneer and Special Constable Humphrey Durrent, who owned a motorcycle combination, and together they set about tracing the criminals. Arriving at Barnby, they soon spotted the pair near the church. As the robbers saw the policemen driving towards them they drew revolvers and loosed off six or seven shots. Poor Mr Durrent received a flesh wound to the leg but the unwounded inspector continued the pursuit as the robbers fled towards Mutford. When he caught up with them, the robbers were trying to burn the money. Inspector Norman had borrowed a firearm, and threatened to fire if they did not give themselves up. Fatigued and no doubt fearing the noose if they carried on, Parsley

Inspector Norman.
(*Suffolk Constabulary Archives*)

and Jarvis gave themselves up. Both robbers received life sentences and brave Inspector Norman received the King's Medal for Meritorious Conduct.

2 FEBRUARY **1856** There was an inquest into the deaths of Willoughby (14) and Jesse Crowfoot (9) at Brandeston. On a cold and frosty day Jesse, Will and their friend Albert Leeds (12) had gone to play on a frozen gravel pit pond. They had hardly made their first slide when Will hit a weak spot and fell through the ice, and his little brother Jesse went to help. Tragically, the younger brother could not lift Will and both were drawn under. Albert grabbed Jesse by his leg and Will by his arm but when his legs went in too he lost his grip, scrambled out for his life and ran for help. Despite willing help from passers-by and from staff at Brandeston Hall, it was too late, and over three-quarters of an hour passed before the lifeless bodies of the boys were retrieved from the icy waters.

Ipswich Town Hall and Post Office, *c.* 1905.

1879 A piece of stone fell from Ipswich Town Hall killing Mr R.J. Davey.

Suffolk beliefs and omens that warn of the approach of the Angel of Death

Suffolk churches would be scrupulously cleaned by this time in February every year, for if every remnant of Christmas decoration was not cleared out before Candlemas Day (the Purification, 2 February), it was believed there would be a death that year in the family occupying the pew where a leaf or berry was left. It was even known for the village gentry to observe this custom to the extent that they would despatch a keen-eyed servant to check family pews were freed from danger on Candlemas Eve.

1892 The results of the second post-mortem of Frederick William Friend were published. On 19 December, Frederick Friend, who lived with his parents on Felixstowe Road, Ipswich, passed away, the doctor giving the cause as meningitis. In the aftermath, and mourning for their son, the parents recalled how, three weeks before his death, Frederick had returned home complaining of having received a heavy blow to his head, delivered by William Norton, which broke his hat. The following morning Frederick had woken up with a stiff neck and a headache; before his death he had been delirious and so violent he had to be tied to his bed. Eventually thoughts and concerns turned to actions and an exhumation was ordered.

The skull was given detailed examination by surgeons Pettingill and Elliston. Their report concluded 'a severe blow would cause meningitis but there was no evidence to show this was the case'. Mr and Mrs Friend thanked the coroner and said that they could now let their son rest in peace.

6 FEBRUARY   **1824**   Adverts were published by B. Brame, agent for the annual meeting of the Ipswich Association for Prosecuting Felons and other Offenders at the Golden Lion, 'when and where Subscribers and other persons desirous of joining the said association are requested to attend'. Before the days of a formal county police force, such associations worked to track and prosecute felons by printing bill posters with rewards offered to informers. Upon information given or evidence presented, the members of the association would then inform the local magistrate and the parish constable would be dispatched with an arrest warrant.

7 FEBRUARY   **1871**   In the early hours of the morning of 7 February a serious affray with poachers occurred on the land owned by Miss Bridgeman at Coney Weston. Four of her keepers were in a wood at about 4 a.m. when they spied a gang of six poachers coming from the lands of Mr Thornhill. On trying to apprehend the miscreants, the keepers were met with a hail of stones, several of which met their mark. One of the keepers managed to get his hands on one of the poachers but was instantly attacked by two of the others – one of whom levelled his gun against him while the other aimed a blow at his head with the butt of his gun. Luckily the keeper warded off this blow with his arm. Backing off slightly, the poachers threatened to shoot anyone who came near them, and then turned tail and ran into the gloom. The keepers stayed back; although the poaching gang had their faces blackened, the keepers had been close enough 'to recognise them as well known and determined breakers of the game laws'.

8 FEBRUARY   **1555**   Dr Rowland Taylor, Rector of Hadleigh, was burnt on Aldham Common. Born in Hadleigh he was lucky enough, once instructed in Holy Orders, to obtain a place as rector of his 'home' parish. He was a well-liked priest who loved his parish well. During the religious wrangles of Queen 'Bloody' Mary Tudor when she realigned the country's faith to that of the Church of Rome, another priest came to say Mass at Hadleigh Church under armed guard. Dr Taylor was locked out of his own church, but finding his way in he accused the officiating priest of being an idolator.

After an extremely vicious exchange of words Taylor was dragged from the church in front of his wife, who begged for mercy on him. Thrown into gaol and put on trial in London, Taylor would not be shaken from his faith to follow the practices of the Church of Rome. He was charged and found guilty of heresy. Returned to Hadleigh for execution as a warning to any other dissenters, he was taken to nearby Aldham Common for burning at the stake. A small memorial still marks the site of this hideous execution.

Dr Taylor's memorial, erected where he was burnt, on Aldham Common.

1934 *First day of the Wortham Tithe War.* In one of the most bizarre actions in Suffolk during the twentieth century, in what should have been a localised incident, a Wortham gentleman farmer, Mr R. Rash, had refused to pay his tithes under protest, and the county bailiffs moved in to seize and impound 134 pigs and fifteen bullocks from Rash's farm. Hearing of his plight and in search of a cause, about fifty of Sir Oswald Mosley's Blackshirts descended on the farm under the command of their National Political Officer, Richard Plathen, hoisted their black flag beside the union flag, and made plans to thwart the removal of the livestock by mounting vigilante patrols and fortifying the farm with barbed wire and obstacles. These actions were unprecedented and thousands came to see from all over the country. Police were called in not only to check the Blackshirts but to deal with the congestion on the country roads. On the afternoon of 17 February, the police were charged with effecting arrests and about 100 officers arrived at the village in two buses. The Blackshirts took up their defensive positions and taunted the police but arrests were carried out peacefully, much to the bewilderment of the onlookers. At dawn on 22 February a convoy of lorries, county bailiffs and police arrived at the farm equipped to tackle all of the fortifications. The police linked arms to restrain the crowd, clods of earth were thrown and a few helmets knocked off but within two hours the cattle

9 FEBRUARY

SUNDAY PICTORIAL, February 18, 1934.

SUNDAY · PICTORIAL

SALE VASTLY IN EXCESS OF ANY OTHER PICTURE NEWSPAPER

No. 988   Registered at the G.P.O. as a Newspaper.   SUNDAY, FEBRUARY 18, 1934   Twopence

FREE HOLIDAY CRUISES SEE PAGE 32

Wireless Programmes on Page 23

TITHE WAR BLACKSHIRTS ARRESTED

Remanded on Conspiracy Charge

Police yesterday escorting to a waiting motor-bus members of the force of Blackshirts who had stationed themselves at a farm at Wortham, Suffolk, where cattle and pigs had been impounded for tithe. Eighteen Blackshirts were arrested and remanded in custody for eight days after being charged at Eye Police Court with "conspiring to effect a public mischief." Bail was refused.

WEDDING ECHO OF LAWSUIT

Miss Gwendoline Fox, sister-in-law of Mr. Harold Bevir, the plaintiff in a recent slander action against Miss Dallas Burt-White, leaving Hendon Parish Church yesterday with her bridegroom, Mr. P. W. Hayden. Right: Mr. and Mrs. Bevir attending the wedding. Miss Fox was a witness in the lawsuit.

Blackshirts posted in a tree as look-outs. Police searched the Blackshirts' hut and took away a signal rocket.

(Suffolk Constabulary Archives)

were removed and the Wortham Tithe War, the only time the Blackshirts went 'into action', was over. The events had drawn national attention but all that remains today is a squat pillar at the junction of lanes above the church bearing the enigmatic legend, 'The Tithe War. 134 pigs and 15 cattle (value £702) seized for tithe February 22nd 1934.' Tithes were eventually abolished in 1936.

1787 A gravestone in Holy Trinity Church, Bungay, reads 'To the memory of Henry Scarles who was valued when alive, and respected now dead, was cruelly murdered at Whitacre, Burgh on 10th of February 1787 in the 23rd year of his age.' According to contemporary accounts Scarle was a servant of Mattias Kerrison, a merchant at the staithe at Bungay. On that fateful night William Hawke of Beccles and Thomas Mayhew of Bungay, with accomplice Simon Stannard, set about robbing one of Kerrison's corn lighters and were disturbed by Scarles. Fired up by the situation, the robbers set about beating Scarles, pushed him into the water and struck him on the head with a quant while he was struggling. Laying low in the locality for a short time they were apprehended at Botesdale by 'persons employed by the Bungay Association'. Taken to Norwich Castle, Stannard turned King's evidence and saw Hawke and Mayhew stand trial, be found guilty and hanged on Norwich Castle Hill the following March. — 10 FEBRUARY

1892 At 4.22 p.m., just before the 'Up' train left Ipswich station, a bullet 'whizzed' through the crowd on the platform. Although it missed everyone, there were many eligible 'targets' on the station that day. They included the Bishop of Ely and a number of magistrates who had just attended the funeral of one of their fellow office-holders. The actions of the station staff are recorded as 'having tracked the author of the mischief who was taking his seat in the carriage – asked to furnish an explanation he produced a six-chambered revolver, claimed it was given to him by a friend and that he didn't realise it was loaded. . . . He gave a card with the name of R.W. Douglas with an address on Fleet Street.' He was quite obviously adjudged a gentleman with no criminal intent, and was apparently allowed to go with no further action taken and a personal apology for any inconvenience from the stationmaster! — 11 FEBRUARY

1499 Ralph Wilford was executed by hanging at Tyburn. Brother Patrick, an Augustinian friar of Suffolk, instructed one of his scholars, Ralph Wilford, the son of a shoemaker, to assume the character of the Earl of Warwick (nephew of Edward IV and Richard III), who was currently imprisoned in the Tower of London. His pretence was effected by saying he had escaped with the aid of Friar Patrick. The story soon received a popular following but Henry VII could countenance no more pretenders or Yorkist conspiracies so his action was swift. Friar and boy were arrested; the Friar was imprisoned for life and Wilford went to the 'Tyburn Tree to become a gallows apple'. — 12 FEBRUARY

1881 An account was published of the recent trial of William Bear, a Sudbury silk weaver charged with killing his son William (10) the previous November. The Bears were a large but poor family. Young William was — 13 FEBRUARY

Borough of Ipswich.

NOTICE
Is hereby given,

THAT the Watch Committee for the Borough of Ipswich, in the County of Suffolk, appointed under the provisions of the Act, " for the Regulation of Municipal Corporations in England and Wales," have appointed the following persons to act as Constables within the said Borough, and such other Places as in the said Act is mentioned---namely:

CHARLES EDMONDS
ROBERT HAYWARD
JAMES RUDLAND

JAMES BARKER	JAMES CARTER
JOHN KEEBLE	ABRAHAM KENT, Jun.
JAMES CLARKE	JOHN PITT
WILLIAM OSBORN	JAMES RUSSELL
HENRY BETTS.	STEPHEN SIMPSON
EDWARD GOSLING	JOHN SMITH
GEORGE EDWARDS	JAMES BARKER, (Shoe-
CHARLES WORLEDGE	maker.)

AND NOTICE
IS HEREBY GIVEN,

That the said Constables so appointed, are to begin to act on Tuesday the first day of March next ensuing the date hereof.

And Notice is hereby further given

That all Watch-houses and Watch-boxes within the said Borough, and all arms, accoutrements, and other necessaries, which have been provided at the public expence for any Watchmen, Constables, Patrol, or Police, in the said Borough, are to be given up to the above named Charles Edmonds and Robert Hayward, for the use and accommodation of themselves and the said Constables appointed as aforesaid; and of such other Constables as shall be appointed under the said Act.

Dated this 13th day of February, 1836.

(Signed)

Robert Root, Printer, Cornhill, Ipswich

employed by James Lumley to assist him hawk fish. On the afternoon of 11 November 1887 a local beerhouse keeper named Charles Butcher had captured the young lad after receiving intelligence he had stolen a purse. He put a rope around the boy's waist and at length the boy confessed. Butcher then sent for the boy's father but his mother came to collect him. At 10 p.m. the same night William Bear senior put a rope around his son's neck and led him to Sudbury Town Hall where he approached Police Sergeant Herbert stating: 'I want you to lock my son up.' After discussing the matter Sergeant Herbert suggested Bear had best 'take the boy home and correct him'. Herbert told the boy he had been cautioned and if he was brought there again 'they had some new birch rods coming from London and they would tickle him with one'. Taken home, the boy was 'spanked about the head' and when he rose on 13 February, he was tied about the waist with a butcher's knot attached to a peg about 6ft from the floor – the idea being to stop the boy sitting down. During the morning Mr Grimwood, the gas works manager, came round to chastise the boy about meddling with gas lamps on the Melford Road. Later in the day William Bear senior went upstairs to look in on his son. He found the boy with his feet on the floor and his back to the door: the rope had slipped up to his neck and a 'ruttling noise' was coming from his throat. The boy was brought down but, appearing to go into a fit or faint, he died. His father was brought before the courts on charges of manslaughter. Bear was found guilty but mitigating circumstances were considered. The judge commented, 'I am told it has been a common practice in the place where you live to punish children by tying them up, the sooner that is discontinued the better for all' (see 23 March). Bear served a sentence of nine calendar months with hard labour.

A traditional Suffolk Valentine's poem   14 FEBRUARY

Good Morrow, Valentine,
Change yar luck an' I'll change mine.
We are raggety, you are fine,
So pray gon us a Valentine.

Good morrow, Valentine,
Curl yar hair as I curl mine,
One before and two behind.
An' pray gon us a Valentine.

1909   Margaret Mary Moult, known to her convent sisterhood at East   15 FEBRUARY
Bergholt Nunnery as Dame Maurus, had tired of life in the religious house and felt trapped so she slipped out of the gate and fled, first to Manningtree and thence via train to her home in Camden Town, London. Her story hit the headlines and despite pressure from the Church she never returned to her nunnery. Within two years she was married to Mr Page and penned her life story, *The Escaped Nun*, which became a bestseller.

16 February

Suffolk Old Dame's Leechcraft

To cure hernia in young children, split a young ash-tree, and pass the child through it naked as the day it was born. Do this thrice at sunrise with the head towards the rising sun; then bind the tree tightly so it may grow together again.

———••———

To cure wens or fleshy excrescences, pass the hand of a dead body over the part affected on three successive days.

———••———

To cure hysteria or epilepsy in a young girl, beg a sixpence from each of nine unmarried men without telling them the purpose of your calling and make them into a ring to be worn on the fourth finger of the patient's left hand.

17 February

1939 *Borley Rectory was burned down.* This sleepy village on the Suffolk–Essex border drew national attention in 1929 when poltergeist activity was reported at the rectory. When the Revd Lionel Algernon Foyster and his wife Marianne moved into the rectory in 1930 the activity increased to the extent 'Marianne Get Help' was scrawled on the wall by invisible hands. Help was sought from the founder of Britain's National Laboratory of Psychical Research – Harry Price. Following the work of Price, and with media hype, Borley Rectory was proclaimed 'The most haunted house in England'. Much has been debated about what psychic phenomena were actually found – some even claimed to have helped Price manufacture the ghosts of Borley. Nonetheless, when the fire of 1939 raged in the rectory, some claim they saw a young girl at the window. The village policeman had the figure of a grey nun reported to him. In 1943 an excavation revealed a female skeleton and religious pendants under the rectory. Photographs of the ruins showed a brick in mid-air, and mysterious lights brought air-raid wardens running before the war was over. Nothing remains of the old rectory today.

18 February

County Bridewells and Prisons visited by Prison Reformer John Howard

Ipswich Bridewell was visited by Howard in 1774, 1776, 1779 and 1782. He found three or fewer prisoners on each visit. The building consisted of a ground-floor work-shop and nightroom for the men, with an upstairs nightroom for women and a court-yard. Howard noted that none of the rooms was secure, nor 'were the clauses against spirituous liquors hung up'. The keeper was a worsted manufacturer on a salary of £17; he was not going to let prisoners sit idle when they could provide labour so he set them tasks of spinning worsted and turning a twisting mill.

1909   A case was reported of a brutal attack at Hartismere Workhouse. An aged inmate named William Kellock of Eye was severely attacked by another inmate with a night vessel and sustained serious injuries to the head and face. The alarm was raised and the assailant, who had twice previously been confined in a lunatic asylum, 'was secured'. Dr Barnes was summoned and attended to Kellock, and the 'poor demented fellow who attacked him' was removed on the following day to the County Asylum.

1819   The appointment of the Bungay Watch (a localised forerunner of the police force) – between 20 February and 1 May the watch was to be maintained every night from ten o'clock until five in the morning. A parish constable was to superintend them. These watchmen were paid 14s a week and the constable 2s a week. Lanthorns and alarm rattles were supplied by the council – all were to find their own candles!

1892   A double fatality occurred of a peculiarly distressing character. Mrs Auger, wife of Mr A. Auger, the proprietor of an eating-house on Foundation Street, Ipswich, was awakened at 3.15 a.m. by her husband's death rattle. She shouted for help to her brother, Frank Smelt (28), who was sleeping in an adjoining room. When he arrived back with the doctor, Mr Auger was already dead. About 8 a.m. Mr Smelt showed the dead body to two men who had called in for tea. A short while later they heard 'a noise like an engine puffing out steam'. Racing upstairs one of the customers (Henry Watson, a journeyman butcher) saw Smelt sitting on his bedside with his throat cut 'almost from ear to ear' and a razor in his hand. The windpipe severed, he died in less than a minute. At the inquest he was said to be under notice from his employer and 'weighed down with grief'. The jury delivered a verdict of suicide while in an unsound state of mind.

1868   The people of Wickham Market come to terms with the discovery of a ten-month-old child drowned in a river leading to a decoy in the adjoining parish of Campsey Ash. The culprit was the child's mother, Clara Coleman. Recently released from Melton Lunatic Asylum she had returned to her parents' home where they watched her constantly. One evening she appeared to go to the privy with the child but was gone a great deal of time and just as a search was about to be instigated, she returned in a shocking state, her clothes saturated with dank water and her hair a mess of brambles, but no child. The search was commenced and Inspector Durrant discovered the child in the water. At the inquest a verdict of 'wilful murder' was given but the jury also agreed they had no doubt of her insanity. At the March Assizes, Clara was ordered 'to be kept in custody until Her Majesty's pleasure be known'.

1872   The inquest was held before the Bury St Edmunds coroner on the body of Robert Wham, an elderly man who kept a small shop on St John's Street. The deceased had been found with a leather strap wound twice around his neck and attached to a beam in the shop. He had been dead for two or three

ESTABLISHED 28 YEARS.

Funeral Car with violet

Fittings & Pall to match.

ROBERT SENTON,
ECONOMICAL
FUNERAL FURNISHER,
PORTMAN'S RD., IPSWICH

R. S. takes this opportunity of informing the Public that
he has now added to his Establishment a splendid new
Funeral Car, which may be had at half the usual charge.

FUNERALS of all Descriptions Furnished in both
Town and Country.

Shillabeer's Funeral Carriage, Broughams, &c.

Branch Establishment:—
Monumental Stone and Marble Works.
BARRACK CORNER, NORWICH ROAD.

Every description of Plain and Artistic Work in Marble, Stone, and
Granite most neatly executed.
**A nice Selection of Monumental Stones on view, to which
I invite Inspection.**
DESIGNS OF ALL DESCRIPTIONS FORWARDED ON APPLICATION.

Manager ... **Mr. F. GREENWAY.**

Advert for Robert
Senton, the
'Economical Funeral
Furnisher', 1885.

days. His feet were 'touching' the ground but the knees were bent and he
appeared to have been apprehensive as to his own weight being sufficient to
cause death so he had attached a 4lb scale weight to his body; 'but what was
more remarkable was that he had previous to suspending himself by the
strap, run a piece of wire, taken from a ginger beer bottle, through his nose
and fastened it to a hook that was hanging from a nail in the beam'. The jury
concluded 'suicide while in a state of insanity'.

1864   Julia Brown (19) of Felsham was arrested on suspicion of poisoning her illegitimate son, Frederick. It appeared she had contrived a meeting with Benjamin Dempster, her ex-boyfriend, having administered oil of vitriol to young Freddy, it was alleged. She knew she would be out of the crowded house she shared with the rest of her family when he fell ill. Dr Leech was called and arrived to see the poor boy in a dying state; he was pale and finding it hard to breathe. His lips were brown and shrivelled and his tongue looked as if it had been rubbed with caustic. During the post-mortem Frederick's stomach was tested for poison by Dr Image who found the presence of sulphuric acid, the same acid which had burnt away some of the material on one of Julia's dresses. Julia's employer's wife, Mrs Betham, stated she had a bottle of oil of vitriol for getting stains off tables. On her return from a few days away during which the murder occurred, she noticed it missing. Julia's ex-boyfriend, Dempster, was no help – stating barely the facts of their 20-minute meeting on the night in question and pointing out he had asked to break off their relationship a month previously. Since Julia was unable to afford her own counsel the under-sheriff appointed Mr Cherry to defend her. In a strong defence Cherry proved the child was no financial burden to Julia, no sulphuric acid could actually be traced to her possession, the dress could not be proved to be Julia's and even if it was the acid burns could have been caused in the course of her work as a maid. The seeds of doubt were well planted and the jury simply could not convict her 'beyond reasonable doubt': a verdict of 'not guilty' was passed.

24 FEBRUARY

1833   The Lynn to Newmarket mail coach had picked up speed in anticipation of overtaking a slower-moving carrier's cart on a narrow road near Methwold. When passing the cart, the wheels of the coach ploughed into a deep drain by the side of the road, causing the coach to topple over. Booty, the driver, was thrown from his seat and crushed to death beneath one of the horses as it fell on him. With passengers both outside and in, it was remarkable that he was the only fatality.

25 FEBRUARY

1888   At the Suffolk Winter Assizes held at Ipswich Shire Hall, Clarissa Ford (17) pleaded guilty to concealing the birth of her child at Ipswich, and was sentenced to be imprisoned without hard labour for a fortnight.

26 FEBRUARY

1792   The inquest into the death of Hugh McNeal, invalid, at the Garrison, Landguard Fort, took place. On the night of 19 February McNeal and a fellow invalid named Mansfield had been drinking at Walton. It had been snowing and drifts had piled up. Setting out into the clear evening the pair were hit by a blizzard. The weather made it difficult to talk and Mansfield thought his pal was beside him as they struggled through the snowstorm but suddenly realising he was not, he looked around but could not see him anywhere. Believing McNeal had turned back to get more drink at the pub Mansfield struggled on back to the Fort. His pal did not return. Mansfield searched for

27 FEBRUARY

his comrade in the daylight but to no avail. McNeal had got lost in the snow and wandered into the marshes where he was found dead a few days later.

28 February   **1888**   This day saw the report from the Suffolk Assizes of a robbery in a house of ill-fame. In a beautifully phrased address by the prosecution it was stated: 'On the night of 5th February, Mr John Roberts, the master of the barge *John of Faversham*, fell in with a woman named Elizabeth Girkin and went with her to her house in Asylum Court.' After he had fallen asleep his watch was put into a cupboard for safety. In the middle of the night John Reeve (29), Girkin's co-habitant, came in and threatened to murder her if she did not turn out the man, but Reeve stormed off. He returned with Jonathan Marsh (23) and they turfed Roberts out of the house. Subsequently missing his watch and the contents of his purse, Roberts informed the police and the items were found on the prisoners. It appears Marsh was acquitted but Reeve, who had a previous conviction, was sent down for five years' penal servitude.

29 February   **Strange and Horrible Tales of Suffolk**

Many folk, on hearing the term 'Sylly Suffolk', assume it refers to the ancient inhabitants of the county being silly rather than to the true meaning of the word – Holy. They are, however, not entirely wrong because the fair county of Suffolk produced at least three renowned court jesters. In Camden's *Britannia* reference is made to Baldwin le Petteur who held lands at Hemingstone 'by the ridiculous serjeantcy of Jumping, belching and farting before the king'. At Wattisham the Wachesham family held the Manor in the reigns of Edwards I, II and III 'by the same indecent service as that at Hemingstone'. Probably best known of the court fools from Suffolk was John Scogan, a native of Bury St Edmunds and jester to Edward IV. His jests were well collected in the sixteenth century. One that has been passed down the centuries dates from when he was given his great house at Bury, near St Mary's Church. His noble-born wife stated she would not be able to find her way to church without a page. 'Poor lass!' cried Scogan, 'you shall have a guide to church before the bells ring tomorrow morning.' The jester rose early and had a chalk line drawn from his house to the church. When the time came to go to church, he opened the house door and with a flourish of his hand towards the chalk line proclaimed: 'There be your guide.' The fastidious lady 'waxed so wrath at the practical trick played by her husband, that all his wit could hardly pacify her'.

MARCH

Mounted police patrol at Lowestoft, *c.* 1905.

1 MARCH **1688** *The Great Fire of Bungay.* Bungay endured its first major fire on 2 September 1652; about 'four-score' houses, barns, maltings stores and stables were destroyed when fire broke out in an uninhabited dwelling and spread with such rapidity that the whole 'burnt to the ground'. Damages in excess of £6,000 were recorded. The Great Fire,

a little over thirty years later, made this look like small beer. With the exception of one small street and a few detached houses, the town was reduced to ashes within six hours. The fire was so intense even the church bells melted. The property destroyed was estimated to have been worth about £30,000 (an incredible sum in those days); it comprised 190 dwelling houses, a church, the free-school, three almshouses, two ancient market crosses and various barns, stores and warehouses. Bungay rebuilt and remodelled itself as a spa (on Bath Hills). The Butter Cross was erected in 1689 in commemoration of the fire. This cross was equipped with a 'cage', restraints and whipping-post for local ruffians, drunkards and petty criminals. Its symbol of judicial authority – a lead statue of Justice, complete with scales and sword – was added in 1754.

2 MARCH **1901** *Discovery of a Strange Drowning Tragedy.* Robert Richer (28) and Edgar Hardwick (18) had not turned up for work and spent the day at a pigeon-shooting match at Otley. They spent the evening at the Nelson Inn, Ashbocking, drinking ginger beer, and left with acquaintances at about 10 p.m. They were seen proceeding in the opposite direction to their homes and this was the last time the pair were seen alive. On this day Mr Tricker of Ashbocking discovered the two bodies in a small pond by the main road. The two men were effectively strapped together by two belts, both men facing the same way, Hardwick having his back to Richer. The bodies were searched but no clue emerged apart from witness testimony to Richer's 'funny schemes' and his 'not being exactly right in the head'. The jury returned an open verdict on the pair of 'found drowned'.

3 MARCH **1872** *The Lowestoft Smallpox Murder.* During the Suffolk smallpox epidemic of 1872 a local brickmaker named William Warnes had been confined with his family to their home at 64 St Peter's Street. His wife had been first hit but was recovering; tragically, in the preceeding week Warnes himself had become infected. Dr Liston had visited at 10 p.m. on 2 March and reported favourable progress among all afflicted, but noted Warnes was suffering delirium induced by the disease. At 10 a.m. William Warnes, possessed by the delirium, arose out of bed, took a knife and attacked his wife. Miss James, a young friend of the family, was in the house and ran to summon help. On her return she looked in and saw Warnes in the act of cutting his wife's throat. She rushed in, snatched up a babe and ran out again – Warnes throwing a knife after her. The surgeon was soon on the scene but could do nothing – Mrs Warnes' head was almost severed from her body. The situation then presented a problem: Warnes was seriously ill and infectious, and the consequences of his being sent to gaol were unthinkable. In the opinion of the surgeon Warnes was so far overtaken with smallpox he would probably not survive, and nature would probably take the place of the hangman's rope. The coroner's hearing was adjourned accordingly.

1901 At the Lowestoft police court four lads named Sharman, Morter, Larter and Abramson were charged with stealing a jar of jam from the Star Tea Company. All boys pleaded guilty. Superintendent Shipp stated Sharman's mother had died when he was 4 years old. He was taken care of by his aunt, who sent him to the workhouse in October 1899. His father and brother 'declined to have anything to do with him. Not long back he left the workhouse and was discovered sleeping in a rabbit hutch and because of his filth and chilblains his toes were rotting away.' In the interests of the lad, Superintendent Shipp asked to have him sent away. And thus Sharman was sent to the workhouse for a week while arrangements could be made for his removal. Abramson was sent to a reformatory until he was 16, while Larter and Morter were bound over for three months under the First Offenders Act.

4 MARCH

1588 Kathleen Ratcliffe had grown tired of her husband; the people of the village of Bures St Mary all seemed aware of this too, because she had done little to conceal her dalliance with local smallholder Maurice Martin. Matters were coming to a head; Kathleen's husband William, although one of the last to find out, did so and followed his wife on this night to see for himself. Maurice had anticipated this and hid in some bushes on the banks of the River Stour. Whether he was hiding in anticipation of meeting his mistress or as part of a plan to remove her husband (with or without her blessing) we shall probably never know, but he sprang from the bushes and cleft open William's head with a quarter staff. Kathleen and Maurice were soon arrested and charged with the murder. Kathleen was declared an accessory but Maurice appeared at the Bury Assizes, was found guilty of murder and sentenced to death.

5 MARCH

1901 *Account of the Treat for Paupers at Hartismere Workhouse.* 'Through the kindness of Mr Howard F. Woolnough' a magic lantern presentation was given describing Her Most Glorious Majesty, Queen Victoria's reign. At the close, the inmates were supplied with a substantial supper and hearty thanks given to Mr Woolnough and the Master, Mr L. Barling.

6 MARCH

1914 Otto Frederick von Medler, 'the Needham Baron', was incarcerated and faced the consequences of his deceptions. He was sentenced to three years' penal servitude for false pretences.

7 MARCH

8 MARCH   **1872**   A reported case of a daring burglary at the premises of Mr Green the pawnbroker on Guildhall Street, Bury St Edmunds. When tradesmen were making their way to work shortly after sunrise it was noticed that the shop shutters had been taken down, a hole made in the centre square of the plate-glass window and all the watches, chains and rings within arms reach had been removed. Jewellery had been spilled over the pavement. Initial thoughts were that some expert cracksman had perpetrated the deed but it soon emerged that three young local men named Robert Pressland, Herbert Goddard and George King were the burglars. They had concealed the stolen goods in some fields near the cemetery but were unable to 'fence' them. Fear of being found out induced Goddard to tell his father what he had done, the latter in turn communicated with the police and all were sent to the magistrates.

9 MARCH   **1817**   Eighty-four tubs of smuggled spirits were discovered by Excise Officers at Walsham le Willows.

10 MARCH   **1664**   *The opening of the Lowestoft Witch trial at Bury St Edmunds.* Amy Duny (Denny in some accounts) and Rose Cullender both stood in the dock on indictments of bewitching Elizabeth and Ann Durent, Jane Bocking, Susan Chandler, William Durent, and Elizabeth and Deborah Pacey. The main case against Amy Duny was presented by Mrs Dorothy Durent, who stated she had asked Amy to look after her infant child William while she went out; for which service she promised Amy a penny. When Mrs Durent returned she found Amy had given suck to the child despite being instructed not to. A row ensued and Amy stormed off. That night the infant William woke up having a screaming fit. The fits did not abate so Mrs Durent consulted 'Doctor Jacob', a Yarmouth man with experience in the detection and treatment of bewitchment. Upon examination of the boy, Jacob had no doubt and proclaimed him bewitched. The treatment was to hang the child's blanket in the corner of the chimney at night, and whatever was inside in the morning should be thrown on the fire. Come the morning a large toad was found in the blanket and was thrown on the fire where it exploded like gunpowder. The following day news reached Mrs Durent that Amy was stricken in bed with severe burns to her head, legs and thighs. Shortly after this incident Mrs Durent was struck down with a mystery malady which prevented her walking without the aid of crutches. One account states that after sentence was passed on Amy Duny, Mrs Durent was able to discard her supports and walk unaided again!

Rose Cullender had gone to the house of local fisherman Samuel Pacey on several occasions on the same day to buy herrings. Pacey refused to sell and on the last occasion Rose was heard to mutter something. No sooner had she done so, each of Pacey's children started to be seized with fits and agonising stomach pains like the pricking of pins. Sometimes they suffered pain all over their bodies, with sporadic loss of hearing, speech or sight. Other times the children fainted and, coming round, began to vomit crooked pins (up to four a time) which tore at their throats. Cullender and Duny were sent to the assizes before the Lord Chief Justice, Sir Matthew Hale. A selection of witnesses gave their testimony and experts shared their opinions, among them the eminent Norwich scholar Dr Thomas (later Sir Thomas) Browne, who was clearly of the opinion that the children were bewitched. The jury had little choice but to convict Amy and Rose. Urged to confess, the ladies pleaded their innocence to the last when they were hanged in Bury market place on 17 March 1664. They were the last women to be hanged for witchcraft in Suffolk.

1893   A report was published of the dead body of a man found under a bedstead in Victoria Street, Ipswich. About four months earlier a residence on Victoria Street was hired by Harry Chisnall, the former landlord of the Alma beerhouse at Hadleigh. He moved in with his wife, seven children and two van-loads of furniture. The man was addicted to drink and six weeks before the grim discovery the wife and children were seen to move out, with the exception of his fifteen-year-old son. The boy was seen to leave in the morning and only return at night to sleep; he ate in the town. The rent being so in arrears, the landlord obtained a warrant and the boy had to leave. His neighbour, Mrs Hearn, was happy to take the boy in and, fetching a few effects for him, she entered a bedroom he did not normally use. Grabbing the valance, Mrs Hearn 'got hold of what proved to her unspeakable horror to be a leg of the deceased man Chisnall'. He was found lying full-length under the bedstead covered by bedclothes and a coat. By his arm was an empty lamp, a teapot and a lemonade bottle containing remnants of a candle. The whole house was in such a state, the boy did not realise his father was dead under the bed; he had kept coming back each evening expecting to see his father return. The post-mortem and inquest proved Chisnall had died of pleurisy and lung infection after crawling under his bed.

11 MARCH

1790   Jacob Foster of Dunwich departed this life, aged 38. When he was buried in All Saints' churchyard a harvestable field stood beyond. His kin probably never considered his grave would take on greater significance over 200 years after his death but so it has, because the field, the rest of the churchyard and even the church have now disappeared over the cliffs and under the waves. All Saints' was the last of the six churches, three chapels, two monasteries and hundreds of gravestones and memorials which stood in old Dunwich. Thus Jacob Foster's grave exists as the last marked grave from an original churchyard of old Dunwich, a silent sentinel and memorial to the inhabitants of the past.

12 MARCH

Jacob Foster's grave on the cliffs at Dunwich.

13 MARCH   **Strange and Horrible Tales of Suffolk**

An account from March 1745 tells of the swift justice meted out to those who did not 'watch the wall as gentlemen rode by'. Smugglers went to the Beccles home of Henry Hurrell, who was believed to have been an informant. Breaking in through a window, they rushed in and dragged him from his bed. Outside they stripped the bleary-eyed man, whipped him mercilessly, tied his semi-conscious body to a horse and rode off with him. Although a reward of £50 was offered for news of his fate, nothing was ever seen of him again.

14 MARCH   **1679**   William Dowsing the iconoclast died at Laxfield, the village where he was born in 1596. Beside the register entry for his baptism is an unusual note added in 1804: 'This man was by the Earl of Manchester, in the Great Rebellion, AD 1644, appointed Visitor of the Churches of Suffolk, to destroy and abolish all remains of popish superstition in them. There are few which do not yet bear marks of his indescreet zeal.' The Journal of William Dowsing records over 150 visits to town and country churches, when he did far more than sign the visitors' book. Included among the entries are Haverhill, where, among the total of 300 images and symbols on glass, wood, brass and stone that were destroyed, he particularly noted the destruction of a picture of 'seven Fryars hugging a nun'. A typical day's work for Dowsing is recorded thus: 'At Clare . . . We brake down 1000 pictures superstitious; I brake down 200; 3 of God the Father, and 3 of Christ, and the Holy Lamb, and 3 of the Holy Ghost like a Dove with wings; and the 12 Apostles were carved in wood, on the top of the Roof, which we gave order to take down; and 20 Cherubims to be taken down; and the Sun and Moon in the East Window, by the King's Arms, to be taken down.'

15 MARCH   **1757**   Reported in the *London Magazine*, 'An Earthquake Shock at Bungay': 'On Monday last, at two or three in the morning, we had a slight shock of an earthquake, preceded by a rumbling noise in the air. As it happened when most people were sound asleep, it was not perceived by many, but those who were awake were very sensible to it. It was likewise felt at Yarmouth, Diss, South Elmham, Loddon and elsewhere.'

16 MARCH   **1881**   Robert Webb, described as a letter-sorter and labourer, was exposed as a petty criminal and was sentenced after a number of accounts of pilfering and tampering with the Royal Mail. He finally received five years' penal servitude. The contrived position of his hands in the picture opposite is no accident. In the early days of police photography and before the days of fingerprinting, any clue to identify a criminal would be recorded. Many people in the nineteenth century had deformities, tattoos or injuries to their fingers which may have been noticed by the victims of their crimes, so every criminal was photographed showing their hands and outstretched fingers as a matter of course. Our friend Mr Webb here is a prime example; note the end of his middle finger is missing.

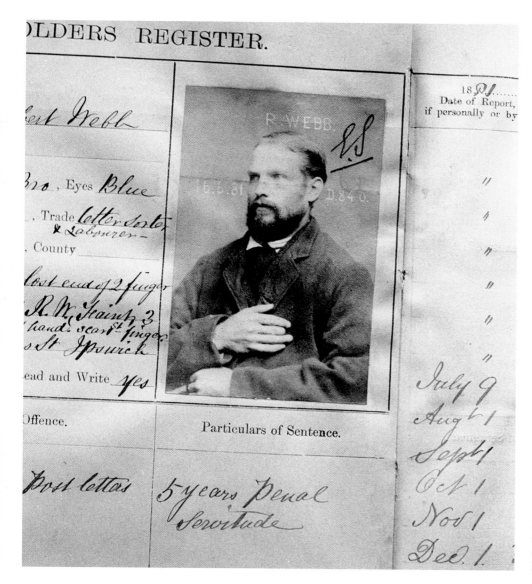

OLDERS REGISTER.

18 91
Date of Report,
if personally or by

...ert Webb

..., Eyes Blue

..., Trade Letter Sorter
& Labourer –

..., County

...lost end of 2 finger

...R W faint 3
...hand: scar 1 finger
...St Ipswich

...ead and Write yes

Offence.

Particulars of Sentence.

...Post letters | 5 years Penal Servitude

July 9
Aug 1
Sept 1
Oct 1
Nov 1
Dec. 1.

Robert Webb, letter sorter and petty criminal. *(Suffolk Police Archives)*

County Bridewells and Gaols visited by Prison Reformer John Howard

Howard described Beccles Bridewell as 'A room on the ground floor, called the *ward*, a chamber for women, called the upper ward, a day room with a fireplace; and a dungeon 7 steps underground.' Howard points out in the ward there was a window to the street 'which is highly improper, as I have always seen numbers of idle persons crowding about it'. There was no proper separation for men and women and only one courtyard. Howard concludes: 'The keeper has a large garden – Salary, £11.10.0. Licence for beer (a riotous alehouse). Clauses against spirituous liquors not hung up. Fees, 6s. 8d. Allowance, a two penny loaf a day [weight in 1792 recorded as 20oz]. Thirty shillings a year for straw. £5 a year for coals. When prisoners work they have half the profit.'

18 MARCH   **Suffolk beliefs and omens that warn of the approach of the Angel of Death**

If the cuckoo gives his note from a dead tree it bodes a coming death to a relative.

———————

If the cuckoo's first note of the year be heard in bed mend your ways or you may not get up again.

———————

The screech of an owl flying past the window of a sick room signifies death is near.

———————

If a bird flies indoors or even taps at the window with its beak the Grim Reaper is at hand.

19 MARCH   **1836**   *George Mann escapes from Woodbridge Gaol.* Having detached an iron spike which had formed one of the bars of his cell (this job had been made very easy because the wood holding the bars turned out to be rotten), he set about removing bricks from the bottom of his cell wall in an area not visible to any warder in the prison. Working hard from about ten or eleven in the morning until three in the afternoon, he removed about 100 bricks. Once this escape hole was clear he dropped down the 12–13ft into the prison garden and was off. He was soon missed and a search was mounted which found him at Witnesham at about 6 p.m. the same evening. The prison report on the incident concluded, 'No blame could be attached to anyone in this matter as the walls of the prison were severely unsound.'

20 MARCH   **1731**   Reported in the *Norwich Mercury* on this day was the case of John Bolton, a Bungay glover who had attempted to cut his throat. Failing in this enterprise, he tried to hang himself but was discovered and cut down before he was dead. Resolved to end his days, Bolton wandered to the river and threw himself in, only to have a well-intentioned waterman see his 'plight', rush to his rescue and successfully pull him out before his life was extinguished. Bolton resolved to live on and was immortalised in an anecdote told by Thackeray (no doubt acquired on his many trips to the area) in his lectures on *The Four Georges* between 1852 and 1856.

21 MARCH   **Strange and Horrible Tales of Suffolk**
In a story recorded by Abbot Ralph of Coggeshall in 1207, a strange merman appears once to have been known at Orford. Recounting events that had happened about forty years earlier, the story tells how fishermen caught in their nets a monster 'resembling a man in size and form; his body was covered in hair but his head quite bald except for a long shaggy beard'. Taken to the governor of Orford Castle, the merman was fed on raw flesh which it 'pressed with its hands' before eating. The beast could not speak, not even

Above: Orford Castle from an eighteenth-century engraving.

when the soldiery of the castle tortured the poor thing by hanging him up by his feet. Brought to the church he showed no concept of reverence or belief. He sought his bed at sunset and stayed there till sunrise. Allowed to go into the sea, the monster seemed at his happiest when diving round the three lines of nets kept in the water to prevent his escape. One day the merman tired of this captive and solitary life in the castle. He swam under the nets to freedom and was never seen again.

One of the wild men on the base of the font in Orford Church.

1179 Of uncertain date is an alleged attack on a young boy of Bury named Robert who was said to have been crucified by Jews in mockery of Christianity. Laws were drawn up against Jews; some of the earliest recorded East Anglian executions are of Jewish elders accused of circumcising Christian babies. Ten years later the simmering pot of hatred against the Jews boiled over and the populace rose against them, attempting to run them out of town. Many were simply strung up by lynch mobs. Several of those who managed to escape were aided by Abbot Samson; those who did get away were banished to return no more.

22 MARCH

23 MARCH **1812**   John and Elizabeth Smith, husband and wife, aged 39 and 27 respectively, were hanged at Ipswich Gaol. Theirs was a particularly horrible case. Elizabeth Smith was John's second wife who inherited John's three children into the bargain – one she did not much care for. John worked hard and came home dog-tired to the family home in Cookley. But no caring parent could have stood by and watched his children starve or done nothing as bruises and weals appeared on their bodies. It emerged from statements made by family members and neighbours that the children were locked in sheds, hung up by their feet or hoisted by a rope around their middles. By this treatment their eldest child, Mary Ann (8), was punished to oblivion. Her tiny starved body could take no more hoistings and she died through lack of food and mortification at the hands of John and Elizabeth. John Wright, the Constable of Halesworth, was summoned; the evidence was all too clear and the couple were taken into custody. At the assizes the jury was out for barely five minutes to find them guilty. The couple were hanged.

MARY ANN SMITH,
Hung up by her cruel Father and Mother, to a Beam in a Shed, in the Depth of Winter, and there barbarously beat and starved to Death!

1864   Letitia Newman (24) awaited trial at Suffolk Assizes in her cell at Bury
Gaol. Newman, a housekeeper to William Keeble, a Baddingham butcher, had
been given notice to quit. As a parting shot she put arsenic into the mug of
porter Keeble was drinking. Fortunately her surreptitious action was noticed
and Keeble was prevented from drinking the fatal brew. Found guilty on 25 March,
she was sentenced to penal servitude for life.

1794   Thomas Hammond appeared on trial at Bury St Edmunds for the
murder of Ann Avery. Her body had been found in a turnip field near
Stanton. Despite being six months pregnant it was obvious she had put up
quite a fight. In a frenzied attack her face had been pushed into the ground
and multiple wounds inflicted upon her body and throat with a sharp knife.
According to the evidence of her sister Mary, Ann had been having an affair
with Hammond and she had seen them talking that morning; other witnesses
concurred with Mary's statement. Stanton's parish constables, William
Stebbing and Edward Clarke, went to see what Hammond had to say for
himself and found small quantities of blood and mud on his clothes – not
surprising finds on farm labourers' clothing in those days. With no forensics
in the eighteenth century there was no way of telling if the blood was human
or animal, let alone its blood type. However, in the absence of any other
suspect Hammond was sent to stand trial. His defence was arranged by his
solicitors – Chinnery and Sparks of Bury. Mr Sparks' cook was the key
defence witness who gave Hammond a cast-iron alibi, and Hammond's
previous employer gave him a glowing testimonial. Even the judge pointed out
the blood on Hammond's clothes was probably from a hog he assisted in
slaughtering the previous day. The jury declared Hammond not guilty – the
killing of poor Ann Avery remains unsolved to this day.

1800   In the early hours of this morning the Suffolk heroine, Margaret
Catchpole, made famous by the Revd Richard Cobbold's book, effected her
escape from Ipswich Gaol. The original notice which offered £5 (rather than
Cobbold's inflated £20) for her capture stated she made her escape at a place
where the spikes of the *chevaux de frize* were broken, reaching it by means of
a garden frame, linen crotch and line. Using these simple aids she scaled the
22ft wall, tied the linen line to the frame of the *chevaux de frize*, slid under the
10in gap left by the broken spike and let herself down with the line on the
other side. The notice concludes: 'This extraordinary escape is only worthy of
such an extraordinary character as Margaret Catchpole, who stole a horse,
and afterwards rode off with it to London, a distance of 70 miles in
10 hours.' For the theft of the horse, she had been tried and condemned to
death at Bury Assizes in 1797, a sentence later commuted to 7 years'
transportation. Margaret was captured again and transported to Australia
where she died unmarried (but not without having received many offers) on
13 May 1819, aged 57. She may have not been the beauty created by
Cobbold, and Will Laud, her smuggler lover for whom she rode to London,
may not have existed but the facts of her remarkable ride, escape and life after

transportation are well-attested truths. *The History of Margaret Catchpole, A Suffolk Girl*, has been reprinted several times.

27 MARCH **1870** Reports were published of the trial of David Heffer (21) and James Rutterford (27) for the murder of gamekeeper John Hight on the Eriswell Estate on 31 December 1869. Hight had been knocked to the ground and mercilessly beaten to death. PC Peck had been on duty just a short distance away that night and had exchanged words with Rutterford and Heffer. When the murder was discovered the two poachers were soon arrested and appeared on trial at the Suffolk Winter Assizes. With a mountain of evidence against them Heffer turned Queen's evidence and saw Rutterford sentenced to death as he walked free. Much to the indignation of local people Rutterford did not keep his appointment with the hangman. Due to a large burn on his face and neck, which caused a malformation, it was considered wise not to 'drop' him and he was sentenced to penal servitude for life. Neither of the murderous poachers evaded death for long though; Rutterford died in prison three years later and Heffer of a 'broken blood vessel' in 1885.

28 MARCH **1814** Maurice Griffin (17) was executed at Ipswich Gaol for the murder of Thomas MacMahon. MacMahon and Griffin had been drinking with a lot of other soldiers. At one point Griffin was rude about MacMahon's brother and a fight broke out, MacMahon gaining the advantage over Griffin. The dispute was broken up and they left the hut. They met again a short while later and the row broke out once more. This time Griffin grabbed his bayonet. MacMahon shouted, 'He will murder me' and ran off across the barrack square. Griffin later passed a group of soldiers; one saw something like a knife in his hand. MacMahon was subsequently found and was attended to by a surgeon but he died a few hours later. In the meantime Griffin had been arrested, denying being out the previous evening, and his bayonet was found to have 2in of blood on the tip. In an open-and-shut case Griffin was found guilty and sentenced to death.

29 MARCH **County Bridewells and Gaols visited by Prison Reformer John Howard**
Howard visited Mildenhall Bridewell on only two occasions. His report was brief: 'Two rooms of the lower 10½ft by 10, and the upper 12ft by 8. No fireplace: no court: no sewer, Clauses against spirituous liquors not hung up. The prison is ruinous; not secure: keeper has a garden; his salary £10: no fees.' Although his comments on Mildenhall Bridewell were brief, he was so moved by the workhouse he had to add a footnote: 'The house of industry, for this parish, situated near the church, was one of the cleanest I ever saw. Here were upwards of forty persons at my first visit, and at my last visit sixty-nine, whose countenances bespoke their satisfaction and the attention paid to them.'

30 MARCH **1540** Following his break with the Church of Rome, Henry VIII oversaw the dissolution and surrender of property from most of the great religious houses of England. For Abbot John Reeve of Bury Abbey his grant of 500 marks and

Constables and sergeants of Ipswich Borough Police, 1883. *(Suffolk Police Archives)*

West Suffolk Police (Bury Division), 1899. *(Suffolk Police Archives)*

a retirement home on Crown Street were no consolation. Many thought his death on this day was the result of a broken heart, shattered by the desecration of his beloved abbey. He was buried close to the abbey in the chancel of St Mary's church.

31 MARCH **1871** *Side Burns.* John Chenery was quite drunk and 'full of the devil'. Rather than return home to sleep it off, he decided to go to church (possibly to exorcise his devil?). He sang his hymns lustily, but tiring of the sermon, decided to liven it up by taking a candle and deliberately set fire to a particularly fine set of whiskers of one of the parishioners. Chenery was brought up before Hoxne Petty Sessions for disturbing the congregation and fined 10s plus costs or three weeks' imprisonment.

TO BE SOLD BY AUCTION,
BY PRIVATE CONTRACT,
AT A REPOSITORY NEAR THE POST OFFICE,
IPSWICH,
BY SIMON NEVERSELL,
ON SATURDAY, THE THIRTY-SECOND INSTANT.
₊ The Sale to begin precisely at five minutes past Ten o'clock in the Afternoon.

LOT.
1　A Copper Cart Saddle, a Leather Hand-saw, two Woolen Frying-pans, and a Glass Wheelbarrow.
2　Three pairs of Pease Straw Breeches, a China Quarter Cart, and two Glass Bedsteads with Copper Hangings.
3　Two Marble Bonnets, a Feather Cap, an Iron Gown, two Straw Petticoats, and three Glass Shoes.
4　Deal Coal Grate, with Paper Smoke Jack, a Mahogany Poker, China Tongs, Cotton Shovel, and a pair of Gauze Bellows.
5　Two Second-hand Coffins with Glass Nails, three Glass Coach-wheels with Cambric Tire, two Persian Saddles, and a Wooden Bridle.
6　A Leather Tea-kettle, an Iron Feather-bed, six pairs of Brass Boots, and a Steel Night-cap.

SUNDRIES.

Pewter Waistcoat, and three Flint Wigs. A Bell-metal Chaff-sieve, and Calimanco Hog-trough. A Buck's-skin Warming-pan, and a Pewter Looking-glass. A Japan Cleaving-beetle, and a Leather Mattock. Three Silk Hog-yokes, and a Pinchbeck Swill-tub. Four Sheep's-skin Milk Pails, and a Wheat-straw Trammel. A Lamb's-skin Grindstone, and a Horse-leather Hatchet. A pair of Pewter Pudding-bags, and a Canvass Gridiron. A Dimity Coal-scuttle, A Wooden Timber Chain, and a Brass Cart Rope.
₊ A few more articles, too NUMEROUS to mention.

PRINTED BY J. BUSH.

A mid-nineteenth-century trick handbill.

APRIL

People of Bury St Edmunds turn out for the funeral of six of the Zeppelin air-raid
victims on 6 April 1916.

1 APRIL   **1916**   *The worst Zeppelin raids on Suffolk.* Zeppelin raider L.16 under the command of Oberleutnant Peterson dropped eight explosives and a pair of incendiaries on Bury St Edmunds in the space of fifteen minutes killing or fatally wounding seven people. The greatest tragedy was suffered by the Durball family. Father was away serving with the Suffolk Regiment when a bomb struck the family home at 75 Mill Road. The bomb killed his wife and two of his children, the other three being nearly suffocated or injured. Hundreds of townspeople, civic dignitaries and soldiers lined the route for the main funeral for six of the casualties of the raid on 6 April. In this same raid Zeppelin L.14 attacked Sudbury, killing five people, while L.13 raided Stowmarket where it was given 'a bloody nose' by anti-aircraft fire and sent on its way, with little damage to the town from the twelve high explosives dropped.

Members of the Durball family, each annotated with their fate, after the Zeppelin raid on Bury St Edmunds, 1 April 1916. *(Original image reproduced in the Daily Sketch)*

2 APRIL   **1851**   James Cadman, William Brown and John Starling of Isleham stood accused at Lent Assizes, held at Ipswich, of the shooting and murder of gamekeeper William Napthen at Elveden. It was alleged Cadman, Brown and Starling were poaching on William Newton's land at Elveden. Witnesses heard the report of a shotgun from the George IV plantation and went running to investigate. Upon arrival they heard a second shot and tracked six men to the boundary bank. The blackened figures in the darkness turned on their pursuers exclaiming 'You bastards, if you don't go back we'll shoot you.' Napthen tried to rush the rogues but a shot was discharged and he went down; two more shots followed wounding Isaac Allen, assistant gamekeeper. The dark figures then ran off towards Eriswell. The case hinged on identification, and because of the blackness and turned-up collars of the poachers, unequivocal identification was rendered impossible and a verdict of not guilty was returned.

3 APRIL   **1815**   Sarah Woodward (25) of Frostenden, executed for murder at the County Gaol, Ipswich.

1766 Betty Burroughs was executed at Bury for the murder of Mary Booty. On 8 March 1766 the body of Mary Booty was found by Bury bellman, Samuel Dixon, near the Risbygate corner of Cornhill in Bury. There was a wound to her forehead which had been delivered by a sharp instrument and a skull fracture running from ear to ear caused by a blunt instrument. Her master, respected local auctioneer Henry Steward, and his mistress, Betty Burroughs, were questioned and soon arrested for her murder. Henry and Betty had eaten a meal and drunk well at the Duke's Head. On his return Henry had entered the house and gone straight out to the backyard to prepare a dressing for his ulcerated arm. Mary Booty and Steward's apprentice George Cowlinge thought robbers had broken in, and armed with a poker and knife, they went to investigate but soon realised it was only Steward. Betty, meanwhile, climbed the palings outside and entered the house by the parlour window. Mary alerted the house to intruders again. The reason for Betty's secret entry was revealed to be to catch Steward 'in the act' with Mary. Henry called Mary a common whore and said he wanted nothing more to do with her and sent her back out of the window. A short while later Mary came running in stating Betty had hit her about the head. It appears Henry then went berserk and testimony conflicts. Neighbours remember him shouting 'Damn you for a whore' and later heard 'Damn you for a bitch! Why do you make such a noise!' from another part of the yard. Either way the body of Mary Booty was found near the front steps of Henry's house in the early hours of the morning. Despite his suspicious behaviour when informed of the discovery, the evidence was purely circumstantial and the jury acquitted the 'upstanding citizen' but found his mistress, Betty Burroughs guilty and hanged her as she protested her innocence. Henry also protested his innocence to his death bed. Could they both have been innocent? A report in the *Ipswich Journal* on 18 August 1767 stated, 'On Friday last, Samuel Otley, a woolcomber, was apprehended and carried before a magistrate declaring he was the person who murdered Mary Booty.' Upon closer examination he was declared insane.

4 APRIL

1794 Reports published of the execution of father and son John (59) and Nathan Nichols (18), who murdered Sarah Nichols (17) the girl who was their respective daughter and sister. It was claimed the father and brother had waylaid the hapless girl near their Fakenham home on the night of 14 September 1793. Striking her down they ran off leaving her to be discovered the following morning. There were two sisters left, one at home aged 12, the other married, and both gave evidence of their father's depravity. Both father and son proclaimed their innocence to the gallows. The father was particularly undaunted by the gallows. He gave his hat and neckcloth to some persons in the crowd and addressed the crowd before he was 'turned off'. He stated: 'Life is but a short passage, and I am now at the last step; of the crime for which I am going to suffer I am entirely innocent.' After execution the son was sent to the anatomists, his body then boiled and the skeleton removed for future study. The father was hung in chains or 'gibbeted'

5 APRIL

near the scene of the crime which was on land across the border with the nearby village of Honington. After the gibbet fell into disrepair, its wood was used in a local bridge and the body in the cage buried a short distance away and forgotten until it was uncovered during the building of the Honington Aerodrome in August 1936.

6 APRIL 1876 Reports were published on the Belton Murder Trial at the Suffolk Assizes held at Ipswich. The story emerged of how elderly and partially sighted Mr Charles Ives went to the back of his cottage at Belton on 13 January to find his equally elderly wife Hannah lying on the floor. Going to a neighbour for assistance it was soon discovered poor old Mrs Ives was bleeding profusely from the head. She was thought to have fallen and hit her head and neighbours tried to revive her with brandy and rest. She died three hours later without fully regaining consciousness. The policeman on his beat was informed and an inquest was called into 'the accident'. In the meantime, another neighbour, Mrs Elizabeth Swatman confessed to her husband that she had killed Mrs Ives by hitting her on the head with a spade. This intelligence was conveyed to the police and Mrs Swatman was taken into custody. The wounds were found to be consistent with those inflicted with a spade and so Mrs Swatman was sent to the assizes. Found guilty of murder, the death sentence was passed on her but was later commuted.

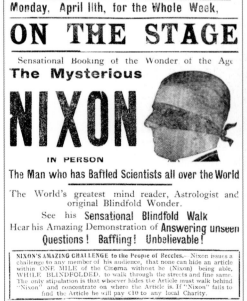

'The Mysterious Nixon' came to Saltgate Cinema, Beccles, in the 1930s.

Alderman Robinson's tomb in St James's churchyard, Dunwich.

1843 The death of Alderman Francis Robinson in his 91st year. His funeral monument in St James's churchyard, Dunwich is in the shape of a great urn and pedestal with raised lettering. This monument is unique, not because it is cast in iron, but because it is the only such monument to have been made by the Garrett Engineering Company of Leiston.

7 APRIL

8 APRIL   **1763**   Richard Ringe and Margery 'Ann' Beddingfield were executed as murderer and accomplice on Rushmere Heath near Ipswich. John Beddingfield was a sturdy yeoman of Sternfield, who had married Ann while in his early 20s and they had two children together. Life was quiet and simple but this did not suit Ann who sought excitement in the arms of another, a farm labourer named Richard Ringe. Soon they wanted rid of Beddingfield and between them devised plans for his demise. After abortive attempts at poisoning, they made sure the master was in his room, sound asleep after a night drinking with his friends. Ringe slipped in, threw a cord around John Beddingfield's neck and, despite a struggle, managed to strangle him. Panic and incompetence betrayed Richard and Ann. They soon found themselves at the assizes and a guilty verdict was returned. The sentence was prescribed by old law – Ringe would hang for the murder but because Ann had committed the act of petty treason against her husband by plotting and abetting his death, she was sentenced to be burnt at the stake. Conveyed to Rushmere Heath on a single 'sledge', Ringe gave an address warning the assembled multitude 'to avoid the delusions of wicked women, and to consider chastity a virtue'. As he was 'turned off' on the gallows the final twists were made to the ligature which strangled Ann at the stake, the faggots were lit with a burning torch and she was burnt to ashes.

9 APRIL   **1742**   Margaret Cutting (24) of Wickham Market was examined by representatives of the Royal Society. When she was four years old a cancer appeared on the upper part of her tongue which soon ate its way to the root. Mr Scotchmore, the surgeon at Saxmundham, used the best means he could for her relief but pronounced her case incurable. One day when some medicine was being injected into her mouth, her tongue dropped out, the girl immediately saying 'Don't worry mamma, it will grow again'. No tongue grew again but 'a fleshy excrescence' did develop there. When she met the men from the Royal Society she conversed freely, demonstrated she could eat and drink as well as any present, discerned tastes, read a book distinctly and 'sung prettily'.

10 APRIL   **1810**   Rhona Boswell died on this day aged 18. On the following day her 3-month-old son, Elijah, also died. Clarke Boswell, the grieving husband and father, saw to it that this epitaph should be carved on their gravestone in the churchyard of St Mary's church, Helmingham:

> Farewell, dear husband, I bid this world adieu;
> Your child is with me – the Lord hath called him, too.
> Here boast not, reader, of thy might –
> Alive at noon and dead at night.

11 APRIL   **1608**   The quarter sessions were in full swing and the market-place of Bury St Edmunds was bustling when fire broke out on the outskirts of the town through negligence in a malt-house. The winds were strong that day and soon the flames were 'blowing clean over many houses' but the direction of the wind kept the fire to 'the buildings farthest off'. The fire consumed 160 dwelling-houses plus stores and diverse other buildings resulting in damages to wares and household effects to the value of £60,000. Great determination was given to rebuilding the damaged areas, King James himself proving to be a great benefactor by contributing vast quantities of timber.

1760 Thomas Kersey was executed at Bury St Edmunds for highway robbery. He had been persuaded to take part in a plan thought up by James Wilson. Wilson would walk up the road in gamekeeper's garb with a shotgun over his shoulder; when the unsuspecting traveller drew into range, the challenge of 'Stand and deliver' would be issued and Kersey would leap out to relieve the victims of their precious goods and money. Many an unsuspecting traveller was nabbed in this way on the roads between Brandon and Bury until the recidivist pair were caught and brought to trial at Bury Assizes. On a contrived plea bargain, the 'brains' of the pair who had devised the scheme was acquitted and walked free in his gamekeeper's garb, but Tom Kersey ended up swinging, found guilty of robbing 10 guineas from the person of Mr Parker of Thornham.

12 APRIL

1829 Twenty-three-year-old George Partridge was hanged at Bury for the murder of 9-year-old George Ansell. This horrible tale began in August 1827 when 7-year-old Jonas Ansell stumbled across Partridge being intimate with his promiscuous teenage girlfiend. Partridge later claimed he had been given the knife and encouraged to commit the crime by his girlfriend. Poor little Jonas was stabbed in a field at Milden by Partridge and later his girlfriend and her mother moved the child's body to an osier bed where it was found a few days later. Although suspicion fell on him Partridge was not charged. Over a year later his girlfriend's family became greedy and began to blackmail him. Partridge became desperate for money and started petty thieving. By some horrible twist of fate, George Ansell (brother of Jonas) saw Partridge stealing lambs on Woodgate's farm. Partridge seized the boy and silenced him by cutting his throat. Farmer Woodgate found the body of young George a few hours later. Word was sent to PC Thomas Bowers at Brent Eleigh who instantly ordered a search. By chance Bowers encountered Partridge near Langley Wood. Finding a knife marked with bloody fingerprints on Partridge, PC Bowers immediately arrested him. By the time the knife was examined (it had been carried in the good constable's pocket for two days) the stains had worn off. Evidence was thin so Partridge was returned to the scene of his crime where his nerve gave way and he issued a full confession which would send him to the gallows. Only when the trial was over, sentence of death passed and there was no chance of reprieve did Partridge confess to a clergyman that he was also responsible for the murder of Jonas Ansell.

13 APRIL

1847 Some folk are simply not suited to married life; what can prove to be hot passion in courtship can cool to hatred in marriage. This seemed to happen literally overnight for Catherine Morley (17) when she wed John

14 APRIL

Foster in October 1846. Fleeing the marital bed on her wedding night, she eventually returned and appeared to settle down at her mother's house with her new husband. One night after an evening meal of dumplings poor John was soon bent double and retching through the night. When he had not improved by the morning Catherine walked to Long Melford to summon a doctor. By the time he arrived at 5 p.m., John was already dead. The initial impression was death caused by the common ailment, 'English Cholera'. There was a nagging doubt, especially as a number of chickens in the yard where the sick had been thrown were found to have died suddenly. John Foster's stomach was removed and tested by Mr Image, the surgeon, of Bury St Edmunds, who detected a large dose of arsenic. Catherine was rapidly arrested, and at her assize appearance in March 1847 she was found guilty and hanged on this day at Southgate Green, Bury St Edmunds before a crowd of about 10,000. It was also on this day in 1863 that John Ducker was executed for murder before a great crowd in Ipswich – this was to be the last public execution in Suffolk.

14 APRIL   1890   Reports were published on this day of a strange case revealed by an inquest at Fressingfield on the sudden death of an 11-month-old baby. The parents, Mr and Mrs Hammond, swore the child was being minded by her step-grandmother, Mrs Corbyn, who had died the same day. On her deathbed Mrs Corbyn had proclaimed the child would not long survive her. The Hammonds took their baby out for a walk a few hours later and were suddenly horrified by the sight of foul-smelling smoke said 'not to be unlike brimstone' issuing from the pram. Elderly George Corbyn told the inquest jury he 'always believed his wife to be a witch'. The inquest could only conclude death was caused by shock caused by some powerful irritant, though what this was, why and by whom it was applied was never determined.

15 APRIL   1880   John James Neavecy (10) stole four pairs of stockings, value 3s, belonging to Elizabeth Wilton, a widow of 10 Victoria Terrace, Kirkley. Easily apprehended, young John appeared before Lowestoft Police Court on 21 April. James Peto, chair of the bench, commented that the boy was a very badly behaved lad, having appeared in court on a number of previous occasions and it was only just over a week since he had had a few days in prison and had been whipped. He was sentenced to Norwich Castle Gaol for ten days and then to a reformatory for five years.

1915 Lowestoft began to clear up after the previous night's Zeppelin raid. German Naval Zeppelins L.5, L.6 and L.7 had set out in an attack led personally by Peter Strasser, head of the German Airship Division (on board L.7) to bomb targets on the Humber. In reality the Zeppelins raided between Burnham Flats in the north and Blackwater in the south. Henham and Lowestoft received the worst of the onslaught from L.5 under the command of Kapitänleutnant Böcker. Although much damage was done, no casualties were incurred.

16 APRIL

Zeppelin bomb crater at 44 Denmark Road, Lowestoft, 16 April 1915.

17 APRIL **1819** Always a draw for the crowds – a treble drop on the gallows at Ipswich Gaol where local villains Jack Ranson, William Hillyard and Henry Laws were executed for burglary.

18 APRIL **1802** Thomas Keeley (22) of Thrandeston and John Read (25) of Yaxley were executed at Ipswich Gaol for burglary. With literally hundreds of crimes on the statute books carrying the death penalty at this time, it was quite common for the pickpockets to pilfer far more from the crowds assembled to watch the execution than the poor souls on the end of the ropes ever stole.

19 APRIL **1769** Mary Burgess was punished at Beccles for 'profane swearing, disorderly conduct and refusing to come before the committee'. She was ordered to be set in the stocks this day for two hours and 'not to be allowed any dinner tomorrow'.

20 APRIL **1870** George Page, 'the Suffolk Giant', died aged 26. Born and buried at Newbourne, George grew to stand over 7ft tall. Along with his brother Meadows, who stood 7ft 4in, they joined George Whiting's travelling fair in May 1869 and travelled the country being put on show as curiosities. Part of his epitaph reads, 'He was exhibited in most towns in England but his best exhibition was with his blessed Redeemer.'

21 APRIL **1824** The greatest number of convicted felons to be simultaneously dropped on the gallows in Suffolk were dispatched before a massive crowd at Bury St Edmunds on this day. They were John Chenery (23) of Beccles, Benjamin Howlett (23) of Exning, Thomas Wright (26) and Robert Bradman (28) both of Glemsford. Their crime? Burglary.

22 APRIL **1851** George Cant (23) was the last man to be executed at Bury St Edmunds. In the rural village of Lawshall the local people knew everyone and most of everybody else's business. Few turned a hair when young Elizabeth Payne began 'walking out' with local farm labourer George Cant, son of a good hard-working family. On 20 January 1851 the village was shocked by the discovery of her body by a grimy pond. She had received a blow above the right eye and her face was bloated. The post-mortem revealed she had been forcibly held under the murky waters until life was extinguished. Questioned at the time of the discovery of the body, George Cant denied all knowledge of the attack or even knowing of her whereabouts. His behaviour was suspicious and his defence flimsy, based on him having

William Calcraft

fits and blackouts. Found guilty, Cant was sentenced to death. The hanging was carried out in front of Bury Gaol by public executioner William Calcraft. Deathly pale and moaning pitifully, Cant was dragged the final steps to the scaffold. When over the trap, Cant was pinioned and his body seen to be 'violently agitated'. Rope adjusted and cap drawn over Cant's head, the chaplain closed his book, the pin was drawn and the trap fell. A voice in the crowd called: 'Hats off, umbrellas down!'

Bury Gaol, *c.* 1875.

1800 Sarah Lloyd was executed at Bury. On the night of 9 October 1799 a fire was discovered in premises adjoining the house of Mrs Syer at Hadleigh. The fire was obviously a case of arson, with four areas in the building shown as origins of the conflagration. After the fire was extinguished Mrs Syer found that not only were a few of her valuables missing but so too was her servant, Sarah Lloyd. Concern turned to suspicion and a search was made for Sarah. She was soon found at Bury and thrown into gaol. She initially implicated two locally quartered dragoons in her misdeeds; this found to be unsuccessful, she named her lover, one Joseph Clark, who was soon reunited with her in gaol. At the trial the evidence against Sarah was damning and that against her lover so weak he was aquitted. Sarah was a pretty young thing and

23 APRIL

received much popular sympathy and when the tale of how she had been manipulated to commit only the crime of opening the door of her mistress to Clarke, who proceeded to commit his crimes without telling her anything of it before, received such public support that appeals were made for 'royal mercy'. But the crime of petty treason, the betrayal of mistress or master by servant was a crime that was assiduously punished by public example, and this was to be no exception. As the cart carrying Sarah passed through the thousands assembled on the route to the gallows from Bury Gaol, women and men openly wept and after the execution the crowd had to be calmed from riot in a fifteen-minute address by Mr Capel Lofft, the Under-Sheriff of Suffolk. Sarah's sympathisers were not going to let her be forgotten; hundreds of broadsheets telling her tale of woe were sold and a stone tablet warning others of her tragic end was erected on the charnel house in Bury St Edmunds graveyard where it may still be seen today.

24 APRIL   **1916**   St Mark's Eve (a popular day for telling fortunes). Suffolk girls would set two inverted pewter pots on a freshly cleaned hearthstone and walk silently, backwards, to bed. In the morning any item found under the pots would reveal a clue as to their future husband's trade; for example, a sliver of wood would suggest a carpenter.

25 APRIL   **1916**   Zeppelin firebomb hell rained down on Newmarket. Zeppelin L.16 under the command of Oberleutnant zur See Peterson made landfall over Norfolk and, having dropped bundles of illustrated newspapers on Kimberley and Thetford, moved on to Newmarket where its bombs damaged over 100 properties and burnt five to the ground. Only one person was injured and the only death was champion racehorse Coup de Main, killed in its stables on Bury Road.

26 APRIL   **1824**   After instigating a bill poster appeal offering a £10 reward for information about who stole his shotgun, Charles Freeman (a member of the Ipswich Association for Prosecuting Felons and Other Offenders), received intelligence that the culprit was one James Lockwood, and saw to it he was put into gaol by the parish constable. After presenting the case to the Stowmarket magistrates on this day, it was heard at Ipswich Quarter Sessions at the end of the month. Found guilty, Lockwood was sentenced to 12 months' imprisonment and was 'privately whipped'.

BOMBARDMENT of LOWESTOFT APRIL 25 1916. KENT R⁰.
SHELL WENT THROUGH 13 HOUSES TAKEN OUT of BEDROOM UNEXPLODED
NOBODY KILLED OR INJOURED MANY NARROW ESCAPES.
12 inch SHELL WEIGHED 8 cwt. 96 lbs. H. JENKINS.

FLIGHT of SHELL THROUGH MIDDLE of HOUSES

Suffolk was not only bombed from the sky – Lowestoft was shelled by German battleships in 1916.

1803   George Jemmett was executed at the Old Bailey for forgery on the Stowmarket Bank.   27 APRIL

1917   Three German prisoners of war escaped from a prison camp in Northamptonshire. Somehow the Germans, dressed in distinctly German civilian clothes and hardly disguising their heavy accents, found their way by train to Halesworth. From there they attempted to walk to Southwold where they intended to steal a boat and sail back to their homeland. On 30 April PC Henry John Seaman was off duty and in plain clothes when he spotted these suspicious characters, then walking on the road from Southwold to Wrentham. Stopping to question the men, he soon concluded they were at least 'aliens' and possibly spies. Arresting all three, they came quietly to Southwold police station and the bold apprehension of the three runaway Germans by a rural Suffolk bobby became national news.   28 APRIL

1907   A horrible fatal accident occurred on this day. Eighteen-year-old George Crane had his head crushed by a steam roller on the Norwich Road, Ipswich.   29 APRIL

1915   *The first Zeppelin raid on Bury St Edmunds.* German Army Zeppelin LZ38 under the command of Hauptmann Erich Linnarz crossed the coast at Felixstowe and, dropping a few incendiary bombs at Ipswich, then navigated   30 APRIL

Above: The burnt-out shell of Johnson Brothers, Buttermarket, Bury St Edmunds, 30 April 1915.

Right: Over 40 Zeppelin incendiary bombs were collected by police in Bury after the raid.

up the main road to Bury where at about 12.35 a.m. it dropped its first bombs. While it was circling the town for about 20 minutes it seemed only half the populace took cover in cellars while the rest could not resist observing the progress of the Zeppelin. Almost fifty bombs were dropped causing damage to a number of properties but most bombs simply burnt out causing no damage or were dowsed by buckets of water. The most significant damage was suffered by business premises on the Butter Market where Day's Bootmakers and adjoining shops were gutted and burnt till morning. By some miracle there had only been one casualty – a collie dog belonging to a Mrs Wise.

MAY

About to dive in for the 88-yard uniform race are constables of Ipswich Borough Police
at the Swimming Gala, Stoke Bathing Place, 1910.

1 MAY   **1648**   On the traditional day of Mayday celebrations when the popular holiday was abolished the people of Bury were not going to be overruled without a fight. About 600 people gathered together and raised a Maypole proclaiming it done 'For God and King Charles'. Raiding the local magazine and laying hold of sympathetic trained bands, the mob manned defensive positions across the town. News rapidly reached Sir Thomas Fairfax, who sent Colonel Whalley to quell the disturbance. After a brief fracas between scouting parties, when two townsfolk and two horses were killed, two Members of Parliament – Sir William Barnardiston and Sir William Playters who had travelled down with Colonel Whalley – bravely approached the rebels. The MPs offered the rioters a chance to lay down their arms, submit themselves to parliament and restore the magazine they raided – they would be pardoned for their 'tumult'. The townsfolk took the easy and sensible option and laid down their arms in the Market House without incident.

An early seventeenth-century May Day.

Last Rites

Joseph's Grave. A mile along the road from Kentford, on the north-east corner of the crossroads where a lane to Chippenham is crossed by the old road between Newmarket and Bury St Edmunds is the grave of Joseph the Unknown Gypsy Boy. The grave is thought to have been here for over 200 years and therein, according to local folklore, lies a young shepherd boy, who having accidentally lost some of his sheep, got it into his head that the consequences would be tantamount to those of theft – namely hanging or transportation. Rather than face an ignominious end on the gallows before a jeering crowd, he decided to take his young life by hanging himself in the woods near the spot where he is buried. This simple grave is tended by passing gypsies and roadmen; when I visited it the fine topsoil had been beautifully combed into a design by somebody's fingertips, some coins lay among the plastic flowers, and a ceramic angel had been placed at the foot of the grave. Around his memorial cross was tied a weather-worn ribbon. Folklore also maintains that if flowers bloom on the grave on Derby Day their colours will be those of the winning jockey (*see* 31 October).

Joseph's grave.

1758 A wager was laid at Newmarket by a young lady that she would ride 1,000 miles in 1,000 hours. She accomplished her feat in little more than a third of the time.

1748 Inscribed on a church memorial at Boxford: 'In memory of Elizabeth Hyam, of this parish, for the fourth time Widow; who by a fall that brought on a Mortification was at last hastened to her End, on the 4th May 1748, in her 113th Year.'

5 MAY   **1910**   Christabel 'Queen of the Mob' Pankhurst spoke on the suffragette cause for the first time in Suffolk at Ipswich Corn Exchange. She was not the

MODERN INQUISITION
TREATMENT of POLITICAL
PRISONERS UNDER A
LIBERAL
GOVERNMENT

ELECTORS !
*Put a stop to this Torture
by voting against*
THE PRIME MINISTER

first national voice of the suffragette movement to speak in Suffolk; that honour goes to her younger sister Sylvia, who spoke in the Ipswich Public Hall in November 1908. The trilogy was completed when their mother Emmeline spoke at Ipswich Public Hall in 1910. By May 1910 public suffragette demonstrations were being held in Woodbridge and Ipswich. In January 1912 Christabel came to Ipswich again; this was the year suffragette movement was to become increasingly militant. Mrs Emmeline Pankhurst was arrested twelve times and Christabel fled to Paris. In Suffolk there were acts of vandalism such as windows being smashed, and protestors disturbed church and political meetings. These incidents were well covered in the local press, and culminated in the arson attack on the Bath Hotel at Felixstowe (*see* 29 May).

At the outbreak of the First World War in 1914 the Women's Suffrage Movement turned its efforts on the concerted war effort and the direct action protests ceased. It is notable that one of the last disturbances caused by suffragettes was at a political meeting with Philip Snowden in attendance at Ipswich on 14 December 1914.

Force-feeding a suffragette!

6 MAY   **1502**   The execution of Sir James Tyrell of Gipping Hall for treason took place on this day. The crime for which he was punished was for helping Edmund de la Pole, Earl of Suffolk, to flee England when his plots against Henry VII proved abortive. Tudor historians would have us believe Tyrell was complicit in a far more sinister crime – the murder of the Princes in the Tower. They allege that under the instructions of the Princes' wicked uncle and guardian, Tyrell supervised John Dighton, his horsekeeper, and Miles Forrest, one of the boys' four tower guardians, as they suffocated the 12-year-old uncrowned Edward V and his 10-year-old brother with pillows so that their twisted uncle could usurp the throne and be crowned Richard III. It is even claimed that under sentence of death for treason, Tyrell finally confessed to this heinous deed.

Opposite: A nineteenth-century interpretation of Sir James Tyrell and his cronies, Dighton and Forrest, glowering over the 'Princes in the Tower'.

There is, however, a tradition in Suffolk that the order was for the Princes simply to disappear and that the Princes in the first instance were removed to Gipping Hall with their mother; rather than being a murderer Tyrell actually helped the boys 'disappear'. Either way, he was complicit in at least breaking constitutional law and it is said the chapel he built at Gipping was erected in expiation of his crime.

7 MAY   **1876**   A prisoner named Reeve, undergoing a term of imprisonment in Bury Gaol, under a commitment from the Ixworth Bench made an escape. He and several others were employed off the prison site in removing materials from the old House of Correction. When the time came for all prisoners to be called in he was found to be missing.

8 MAY   **1853**   *The Bacton Rectory murder.* On this Sunday morning the aged Revd Barker took his young servant girl to church and left Mrs Maria Steggles, his equally aged housekeeper (they were both in their 80s), to cook the lunch. On their return from church they entered the kitchen to discover a scene akin to a slaughterhouse. Poor Mrs Steggles was on the floor, blood from the wounds inflicted on her head and the gash to her throat spattered across the walls, across her open prayer book and smashed glasses. Suspicion immediately fell on William Flack (18), who had recently been dismissed from the reverend's employment, who bore a grudge against Mrs Steggles and had not kept his feelings quiet. He was heard to say he would soon 'steal some of the old parson's mouldy sovereigns'; even before his arrest he was stating he had not meant to kill her but 'she's dead now, so that's all right'. His mouth did not endear him to the assizes either, as he tried to implicate another in the crime, but when convicted he openly confessed he had rung the bells for Sunday service and, having 'chimed the parson in', ran to the rectory and did the deed! William Flack was executed at Ipswich Gaol on 16 August 1853.

Bacton Rectory, *c.* 1903.

1913 A skeleton thought to be of some antiquity caused quite a stir when it was discovered by workmen 6ft below the floor of a house on Dial Lane, Ipswich.

1797 Death of Robert Davy (54), late Master of the Beccles Free School and first master of the Apollo Lodge of Freemasons, who had a magnificent memorial erected to his memory in the parish church by his brethren lamenting his passing as a 'regretted victim to the stone and gout'. Davy could have had his stone removed – it was one of the few operations available before the nineteenth century. Trussed on your back with wrists tied to ankles while the surgeon probed the urethra with a catheter followed by a bigger probe to located the stone. A large incision was then made through the perineum, reaching into the bladder the surgeon could remove the stone. All this was conducted without an anaesthetic.

1884 *Baby-farming scare at Ipswich.* The body of a baby was found by two men named Betts and Brooks, in a pond known as 'Tinker's Hole' on the Westerfield Road, Ipswich. Betts had sent his dog into the water for a bath, and the dog returned with a parcel. A quay porter named Lawrence was passing and opened the parcel. Inside was something wrapped in an old towel; when this was opened, to the horror of all, they discovered the body of a newborn male baby. PC Cobb was soon on the scene with Mr S.S. Hoyland, the police surgeon, who said the body had been in the water a few days. He removed the poor little mite to the mortuary. The inquest returned an open verdict, but it did not take much for local folk to reel off a handful of similar incidents of babies' bodies being found in similar circumstances and the first baby-farming scare hit Ipswich. The second erupted in February 1893 when the abandoned remains of an infant were found on a church wall. This really was one of the most vile crimes, indicative of the hypocrisy of the times in which it was committed. Young ladies found 'in the family way' but unmarried could find adverts or hear through the grapevine of 'nurses' who, for a fee, would place the child with a loving family with no awkward questions, form-filling or embarrassment. It was not until the real fate of the babies was exposed by chance discoveries that this hideous practice was exposed. Only after high-profile trials in London of the likes of 'Nurse' Amelia Dyer, which ended with her execution, did baby-farming became a thing of the past.

1815 *Firing of a barn at Lawshall.* Tensions ran high between farmers and labourers across Suffolk, and Britain in general, as exorbitant prices were commanded for bread flour. Sporadic instances of threshing-machine breaking were occurring and a riot at Gosbeck in the preceeding March resulted in the conviction of nine. Fearing major civil disturbances, magistrates took to strong-arm tactics to maintain law and order. So, when an arsonist struck at Lawshall burning a hay barn, adjoining buildings and animals therein, the law moved swiftly. Suspicion fell on James Pleasants, the young farmboy. James confessed after some cajoling and claimed he started the fire by throwing a burning coal into the barn. He implicated no others. When his trial came he retracted the confession and claimed he had acted under duress from the local protest leaders, which was probably the truth but examples had to be made and James was sentenced to death. Even the judiciary of the time had to admit the lad was not responsible alone for the fire and his sentence was commuted to transportation to the Australian penal colonies for life.

13 MAY   **1748**   Susan Mayhew (5) was murdered by William York (10) at the Parish Poorhouse, Eyke. After a trivial argument between the two children, young Susan went outside the workhouse to the dunghill; William followed her with a hook in his hand. After committing murder and horrible mutilation of the little girl, York sluiced her, and the ground around her with water and hid her body in the dung heap, went inside, had a wash and had breakfast. This young murderer was soon revealed and he stood trial for his crime. Found guilty, he was sentenced to death but was respited on account of his tender years.

14 MAY   **1876**   *Reported fatal accident at Bury St Edmunds.* Samuel Watson, 'a young and sober porter' on the GER station at Bury, was removing the tail lamp from the last train from Thetford, which had been shunted to a siding. At the very moment he was moving away the train was backed up and the poor fellow got caught between the buffers of the last carriage. Fearfully crushed, he was immediately taken to the Suffolk General Hospital. 'He lingered till about one o'clock in the morning, when death put an end to his suffering . . . He leaves a wife and five children.'

15 MAY   **1876**   *Exciting chase at Stradbroke.* A young woman entered Waterloo House and purchased various articles of drapery and millinery, stating they were for Mrs Mutimer of Hoxne and should be placed on her account. The goods were directed to the Queen's Head Inn, where a chaise was said to be waiting. No chaise was waiting; the woman suggested the groom must be driving to and fro to prevent the pony taking cold and asked the assistant simply to leave the goods with her and she would walk up the Wilby Road to meet the driver. The goods were left with her but suspicions had been aroused; an immediate search failed to find her, but with the assistance of a dog she was discovered hiding in a ditch full of brambles. Failing to provide proof of the identity she claimed, she was remanded at Stradbroke Petty Sessions.

16 MAY   **1856**   Bill posters across the county and flyers handed to the carriers and stage coaches were circulated announcing that the Pugilist Championship of All England was to be decided on 19 May near Bentley. It was between Tom Paddock and Harry Broome. The match was attended by the great and the good from far and wide, including local luminaries such as Richard Garrett

A Devil of a fight!

the Leiston Ironfounder, and an Indian prince with his entire entourage. In 1856 the gloves were literally off – it was all bare-knuckle fighting – so the achievement is all the more considerable when the match was decided in Paddock's favour after fifty-one rounds.

Suffolk Old Dame's Leechcraft

17 May

To prevent cramp, wear a ring made out of an old coffin handle on one of your fingers. In the eighteenth and nineteenth centuries many a Suffolk sexton and parish clerk across the county would save handles turned up in graveyards for this purpose.

Another preventative charm for cramp is to carry the patella or knee-bone of a sheep or lamb, carried in a pocket, the nearer the skin the better or laid under the pillow at night. Some hardy folk who were in with their local sexton managed to obtain human patellas – these were considered many times more potent.

To prevent cramp in bed, place your stockings by the bedside in the form of a cross.

18 MAY   **1876**   A small-scale riot took place at Ipswich between soldiers and civilians. Events began when a row erupted between an artilleryman and a local in the White Elm on Bishop's Hill. The soldier's comrades came to his aid with whips and lashes flying; they were met with blows and fists from locals. A large crowd of spectators lined the street to watch the combatants, some of whose faces were streaked with blood and their clothes dusty, as they gradually surged down the hill to the Fore Hamlet. Part of the Borough Police Force which had been on duty at the racecourse happened to be riding by. Police staves were drawn and the rioters engaged. After a brief fracas and a few arrests the riot was quietened, apart from the hoots and jeers from the crowd as the police led the rioters to the police station.

19 MAY   **1536**   Queen Anne Boleyn (left), second wife of King Henry VIII, was executed on Tower Green at the Tower of London. When a carefree young girl she stayed many times with her aunt, Almata Calthorpe, lady of the manor of Erwarton. Local legend told of how Queen Anne made secret arrangements with her uncle, Sir Philip Parker, that her heart be entombed at the Church of St Mary at Erwarton. Such a tale could be easily disregarded as a flight of fantasy had not a small leaden casket, covered with lime and dust, been uncovered by stonemasons attending to a bulge in the south wall of Erwarton Church in 1836. After it was opened only a little black dust was found inside; once soldered up again it was placed on a coffin in the Cornwallis vault beneath the organ. The casket was clearly shaped into the form of a heart.

20 MAY   **1909**   Newspapers across Britain were full of accounts of an unexplained luminous airship seen traversing the country from Wales to Suffolk. To put this event into perspective, the Wright brothers only achieved powered flight in 1903, Bleriot would not fly across the Channel until two months later and the first channel crossings by airship were a year away. Panic occurred in certain quarters; talk of these mysterious Zeppelins led to suggestions that their purpose was sinister. One persistent suggestion was that they were spying for Germany. Mr J.W. Stockman, the skipper of a Lowestoft trawler, stated that when he saw the airship he was some 35 miles from Lowestoft. The third hand called him on deck, and he discerned what at first seemed to be a star rising; he then perceived a cigar-shaped form in the sky, similar to the pictures of airships he had seen; he was confident it was not a balloon. Stockman burned a red flare, which was answered by a red flare from the airship overhead. He then burnt a white flare and the airship answered with a blue one. The skipper concluded that if the airship had carried on its tack observed over the trawler 'it would have ended up to the north of Holland and over Holland to Germany'.

1556 Three Martyrs from the purges of Queen 'Bloody' Mary, namely Thomas Spicer of Winston, John Deny and Edmund Poole, both of Mendlesham, were burnt at Beccles. The case of Spicer (19) was particularly tragic. He had been arrested by Sir John Tyrell of Gipping for failing to turn up at Mass and was thrown into Eye Gaol where he awaited his fate with Deny and Poole. The fateful day came at Beccles 'When they rose from prayer, they all went joyfullie to the stake, and being bound thereto, and the fires burning about them, they praised god in such an audible voice, it was wonderful to all'. But a citizen of Beccles named Robert Bacon took exception and 'willed the tormentors to throwe on faggots to stop the knaves' breaths, as he termed them; so hot was his charitie'.

21 MAY

Queen Mary, nicknamed 'Bloody Mary', after her religious reforms that sent many to a fiery fate.

22 MAY

Suffolk beliefs and omens that warn of the approach of the Angel of Death

The picking of green bloom or May blossoms brings death to the family into which it is brought.

If an apple or pear tree blooms twice in the year you can know for sure death is near.

A bouquet of poisonous flowers and plants.

Taking a sprig of blackthorn, when in blossom, into a house is considered to presage death to some members of the family.

The mandrake plant is supposed to grow where criminals have polluted the earth; it was said to be especially prevalent under gallows where the 'drippin's of felons fingers' made the plant flourish. Witches wishing to predict or 'see' deaths would uproot the plant for their concoctions but not without the greatest care. If mandrake was to be lifted for magical intent it would give an unearthly shriek as it left the earth which, if not guarded against, would induced madness or death to the lifter.

Some of the Tudor shops in Lavenham, *c.* 1905.

23 MAY   **1881**   Miss Caroline Mills (44) died suddenly at Lavenham. At her inquest it was revealed she 'lived poorly and had illegitimate children'. It was remarked that despite help from her family she often had but morsels of bread to live on. Mr W.K. Bourne, the chemist, stated she had come to him with pains and he had given her 'aperient powders and a mixture composed of iron, spirits of chloroform and water, which did her good'. She even had a second bottle of it! Despite the best efforts of local medical men she had 'remained strengthless' and passed away. The cause of death was given as 'a sad case of apoplexy'.

24 MAY   **1893**   A sailor was by fault of a tragic accident blown to pieces on HMS *Mersea* in Harwich harbour.

25 MAY   **County Bridewells and Gaols visited by Prison Reformer John Howard**
Lavenham Bridewell was visited on four occasions between 1776 and 1782; each time there were three or less prisoners except in April 1776 when fifteen impressed men were held there. The Bridewell was found to consist of a workroom, a chamber for men and only one room for women: none of the rooms were secure. Howard commented: 'the prison is out of repair. On a previous visit I heard a prisoner escaped, for which the keeper was fined, though the *neglect* lay in the magistrates. Two more, lately escaped through

the plaster wall . . . Prisoners always kept within doors; the court not secure: no water: no straw'. The keeper's salary was noted as a generous £15 14s 8d and the prisoners kept occupied by spinning wool. Howard concludes: 'There is no proper separation of female prisoners. A old out-house and stable of the keeper's might be convenient for them. At my last visit, I found the *magistrates had sent to the keeper a number of thumb screws for securing prisoners.*'

1881   A man named Thomas Farthing attempted to hang himself with a   26 MAY
halter at Nayland. When he became 'excited and violent' the alarm was raised by his family and acted upon by his neighbour, Mr Southwood. The local police sergeant was summoned and, deciding Farthing was quite unsound of mind, he restrained him and saw him sent to the lunatic asylum. The report concluded: 'Farthing, who is a native of Bildeston, was for several years in the Metropolitan Police force and it is said he met with some rough treatment which incapacitated him from further service and may have tended to produce insanity.'

1881   William Last (59), a well-respected,   27 MAY
conscientious and able shepherd, who had been employed upwards of forty years by two generations of the Mallows farming family of Beyton, left his cottage early on this morning to tend his flock. He had been deeply affected by the loss of three sheep and a lamb the previous day, though he was not to blame. He was found by fellow labourers laying flat in a small pond with about 24in of water in it. It was stated that Last had cut some sallows from the edge of the pond where the bank was 10ft high and could well have fallen in there. The jury returned a verdict of 'found drowned'.

1672   *The Battle of Sole Bay*. Celebrated as an 'obstinate and sanguinary naval   28 MAY
engagement', the Battle of Sole Bay saw the fleets of England and France combined against the Dutch. England and France fielded 101 men-of-war sails plus fireships and tenders carrying a total of 6,018 guns and 34,500 men whereas the Dutch came with 168 vessels, of which 91 were men-of-war. The English and French were laying upon the bay 'in negligent posture'. When one of the naval commanders, the Earl of Sandwich, informed his senior, HRH James, Duke of York, he was censured and his courage questioned in reply. When the Dutch ships approached, he was first out of the bay; had Sandwich not acted promptly, de Ruyter's fireships would have destroyed the combined fleets. This timely action enabled the ships of the Duke and the French to

disentangle themselves and bought them valuable time as Sandwich returned to do battle, determined 'to conquer or die'. Sandwich proved more than a match for the Dutch admiral whom he engaged full-on and slew with his own hand, sinking a man-of-war and three other vessels but, sadly, the shot of the Dutch broadsides slowly decimated his crew and sunk Sandwich's ship. The battle raged on all day and the exchange of fire was declared by many old sea-dogs to be unprecedented. Night saw the Dutch ships disengage and the English declared the victors. The losses on both sides were thought to have been nearly equal – the Battle of Sole Bay was a near-run thing!

29 MAY   **1914**   Suffragettes Evaline Hilda Birkitt (37) and Florence Olivia Tunks (22) were convicted of burning down the Bath Hotel, Felixstowe, on 28 April. Beginning their pyro tour at Great Yarmouth, where they had started the fire on Britannia Pier, following on to Ipswich where they set light to a 120-tonne of cattle feed, the suffragettes made their final target the Bath Hotel at Felixstowe. They always attempted to ensure the safety of others while maximising the impact of their militant actions to draw attention to their cause. The Bath Hotel, empty for its refurbishment in anticipation of the

summer season, was an ideal target. The hotel 'went up like a torch' and little could be done to save it. Luggage tickets bearing suffragette campaign statements were discovered by an attending bobby. Birkitt and Tunks were soon identified as strangers and were arrested after refusing to give their names or reveal their addresses. Soon identified as the arsonsists, the suffragettes (whose conduct in court caused uproar) were found guilty; Birkitt was sentenced to two years and Tunks nine months. True to their cause they did not go quietly and even went on hunger strike while in Holloway. After the First World War these outrageous acts were all but forgotten and these suffragette heroines faded into obscurity and lived to ripe old ages.

1924   The first uniformed Ipswich Police Matron was recruited. The position was filled by 26-year-old Miss Adelaide Bryant, her primary responsibility being the women in custody.   30 MAY

Beccles and Lowestoft District police officers, 1897. (*Suffolk Constabulary Archives*)

31 MAY **1881** Report of William March appearing before the petty sessions at Sudbury for the theft of a gallon of whisky from the Bull Inn. Witnesses stated he was seen coming out of the taproom with a bottle of whisky and promptly leaving the pub. Mary Ann Elliott, the housekeeper seeing this, summoned the tap-boy and sent him after March and he was brought back, with the whisky, to the pub. Found to be in a state of intoxication, he was handed over to the constable. In court March claimed no recollection of the entire incident. The bench were not amused; the Mayor Mr G.G. Whorlow put the blame squarely on March's drinking habits and proclaimed this was, however, 'no excuse' and sent March down for two months with hard labour.

Black crêpe and parasols are to the fore as Sudbury comes out in full mourning after the death of King Edward VII in May 1910.

JUNE

William Harsent sits by his murdered daughter's grave
in the churchyard at Peasenhall.

JUNE The funeral of Billy Twigger took place, a poor unfortunate simpleton who resided for many years at Hadleigh poor-house, where he died in June 1816. His conduct in general was perfectly harmless. At local festivities and special occasions he was 'a constant and delighted attendant'. He was especially fond of military spectacles and when the bands marched through the town, he was always to be seen drumming on his tin-kettle at the back of the parade.

> On batter'd water-pot in lieu of drum,
> With varied measure beat the loud tattoo;
> Press'd through the crowd, regardless of its hum,
> Nor would his clattering melody forego.

He was recorded in several verses on broadsheets and his last sad resting place, a pauper's grave in the churchyard recorded thus:

> Not e'en an osier'd hillock heaves to show
> That the poor idiot, Billy sleeps below.

Poor Billy Twigger.

1902 The murder of Rose Anne Harsent (23) took place at Providence House, Peasenhall. Rose Harsent was a local girl employed at Providence House, the home of Mr and Mrs William Crisp. Her father, William Harsent, came round at 8 a.m. to bring her clean washing. Finding the back entrance open, he stepped inside to discover his daughter lying dead in a pool of blood on the floor. PC Nunn was immediately summoned, surveyed the scene and conducted a search of her room for clues. He turned up a few letters, one arranging a secret assignation at midnight the previous evening. PC Nunn then called his police inspector, who recorded the scene when he arrived at 2.30 p.m.: 'The throat was cut left to right severing the windpipe and left jugular vein the flannelette night dress worn by deceased was partially burned as was also the chemise. A quantity of broken glass was found near the body (from a lamp she was carrying and must have dropped when attacked) as was 10oz Doctor Medicine Bottle . . . (noting the letters found he states) A man named William Gardiner is suspected'. Gardiner (35) was a foreman at the nearby works and a prominent local in the Primitive Methodist Chapel. He was an upstanding citizen, and there were a malicious few who were jealous of him. He was married but local boys had put about a malicious rumour that he and Rose, a member of the chapel choir, were behaving 'inappropriately' together. The gossip-mongers went to work, and in November William Gardiner was on trial at Ipswich for Rose Harsent's murder. The evidence presented did not convince all the jurors and they could not agree – eleven for conviction, one for acquittal. At a retrial in the following January the same thing happened – eleven for, one against. The case was declared *nolle prosequi* – in effect, the law gave up. Set free on 29 January 1903 Gardiner felt he could not return to Peasenhall – his name simply had not been cleared – so he shaved off his beard and disappeared into obscurity in London. The murder of Rose Harsent remains unsolved and a theory has even been put forward that it could all have been an accident whereby she fell down the stairs, gashed her throat on the lamp she smashed as she fell, and set her nightdress alight with the spilled paraffin of the lamp.

DESPERATE MURDER BY LONDON "HOOLIGANS."

THE ILLUSTRATED POLICE NEWS

LAW COURTS, AND WEEKLY RECORD

ESTABLISHED 1864

No. 2000. SATURDAY, JUNE 14, 1902. Price One Penny.

THE HOUSE, IN WHICH THE BODY WAS FOUND.

SENSATIONAL CRIME IN SUFFOLK.
A VILLAGE GIRL'S MYSTERIOUS DEATH.

2 JUNE **1926**   The inquest was held into a triple tragedy at Wickham Market. When Joseph Ward arose at about 6 a.m. on 1 June, he noticed water was running past his cottage door on Smithfield Terrace, just off Bridge Street. Following the trail of the water he found its source was his neighbour's water butt – with his neighbour's legs sticking out of it! Ward ran over and pulled his neighbour, Arthur Smith (56), out of the butt. However he was found to be quite dead and his throat gashed. Ward called into Smith's house for help but nobody came so he summoned his neighbour, James Eagle. Ward went for Drs J.C. and K. Keer and Eagle summoned Police Sergeant King. Entering the house, Sergeant King found a bloodstained razor on the table. Upstairs under his bedclothes and some old coats was Arthur Smith's brother William, his head badly battered and his throat severely cut. A bloodstained axe lay on the bed. In an adjoining room was Arthur's wife, Elizabeth (50). Lying on the bed, her head had been smashed with the bloodstained poker that lay beside her. Her throat had also been cut. No particular event was ever identified as the trigger for this terrible murder but the court agreed that Smith had dispatched his wife and brother, and then, after gashing his own throat, had walked down the garden and drowned himself in the water butt.

3 JUNE **1665**   When thinking of naval engagements in Suffolk, most think of the Battle of Sole Bay (*see* 28 May), but equally significant was the engagement off Lowestoft on this day between Charles II's English fleet and the Dutch. The Dutch fleet consisted of 102 men-of-war, 17 yachts and fireships, while the English Fleet comprised 114 men-of-war and 28 fireships. In a battle which raged between three in the morning and seven in the evening the Dutch ended up being completely routed with 18 ships captured and 14 sunk or burnt. The English lost only one ship and 250 men, the wounded not exceeding 350.

4 JUNE **1894**   At the opening of the Suffolk Summer Assizes Maurice Dyer (24), Harry French (18) and David Deaves (19), all of whom were labourers, were charged with stealing a stick and 2½d in money from Thomas Hayward at Little Coman on 13 April. The judge noted that the men had robbed an old man with considerable violence and their punishment would reflect this. Dye was given three calendar months' imprisonment and was ordered to be 'at once flogged, receiving twenty lashes of the cat'. Deaves received two months and eighteen lashes and French one month and fifteen lashes.

5 JUNE **1583**   John Copping, a shoemaker, was hanged at Bury for 'spreading and maintaining several tenets written by Robert Browne' (founder of the Brownists or Independants). Brown had published three tracts, namely *A Treatise of Reformation without Tarying for Anie*, *A Treatise upon the 23 of Matthewe* and *A Book which Sheweth the Life and Manners of all True Christians*. Published in England separately and in a compendium volume, they were condemned in a special proclamation by Elizabeth I. In that same month Copping and local tailor, Elias Thacker (on 4 June) met their fate for effecting distribution in Bury. Copping and Thacker are remembered on a memorial in the grounds of the United Reformed Church on Whiting Street.

1841 *The first Suffolk policeman shot on duty.* At about 1.30 a.m. an armed and dangerous gang of about ten burglars were robbing a malt store at Higham, near East Bergholt. Two patrolling police constables stumbled on the burglary and all hell broke lose. One of the burglars was arrested but the rest fled. PC Chambers gave chase and was shot in the arm and back causing serious injuries. As investigations were made into the rest of the gang it transpired they were from West Suffolk but unfortunately no formal police force existed at the time across the divide of the county!

1887 The report was released of the inquest at Barton Mills on the body of John 'Whiffy' Rogers (45). Rogers had been a clerk in a dry goods store in New York, and had come to England a few months previously, having been advised by a doctor to do so for his health. Rogers went out for constitutionals twice a day but one night he did not return. His employer, Joseph Palmer, set about looking for Rogers, who he knew to have 'softening of the brain', and to have recently lost himself on two occasions in Thetford. A man named William Bacon found Rogers' drowned body in the river at Mildenhall a few days after he disappeared. At the inquest it emerged Rogers was 'a person of dirty habits' and was nicknamed locally as 'Whiffy'. When his body was discovered it was found to be only partly dressed – it appeared poor John Rogers had accidentally fallen into the water and to his death while attempting to wash his clothes.

1894 A preponderance of mail robberies featured at Suffolk Summer Assizes, held at Bury. Mary Smith (18) was indicted for stealing a postal order to the value of 7s 6d from the postmaster at Stanton. Justice Knight stated Smith 'had shown a great deal of low cunning . . . and for her own sake [he] must give her a term of imprisonment which would give her time to reflect upon her conduct'. He hammered down ten months with hard labour. William Ellis Norman, a postman, was also charged with three counts of stealing letters and 10s in money. As a postal official and one 'who had abused his position of trust', he was sentenced to twelve months with hard labour.

1887 At the Borough Petty Sessions, Bury, a 9-year-old boy named Eley was brought before the court for stealing from the pocket of Sarah, wife of William Winter, the sum of 20s at Bury market the previous Wednesday. The boy was clearly identified by witnesses, who had observed him putting his hand in Mrs Winter's pocket and throwing his booty under a stall, from where his accomplice, Walden, picked up the goods and ran off. Walden was brought up in court, identified Eley but denied being in the Butter Market at the time. Walden's statement does not seem to have been too closely questioned and Eley was left to take all the blame . . . and punishment. The Mayor on the bench told Eley he 'would end badly if he did not reform' and sentenced him to receive six strokes of the birch rod after being kept in prison for one day.

10 JUNE

Suffolk beliefs and omens that warn of the approach of the Angel of Death

If a swarm of bees alight either on a dead tree or dead bough of a living tree near the house, there will be a death in the family in the near future.

———•+•———

If a clock 'loses a stroke' or refuses to go properly, a death will be known to the family.

———•+•———

Three raps on a bed's head is an unwelcome greeting as it warns of death.

———•+•———

The howling of a dog at night in front of your house, particularly near a room where there is a sickbed betokens a death.

———•+•———

Tablecloths and particularly sheets were carefully examined for oval creases known as 'coffin folds' that signified imminent illness or a fatality to the household.

11 JUNE   **1909**   An account was published of Ixworth Petty Sessions hearing the case of two policemen being assaulted at Wattisfield. PC Walter Double having received complaints went to White Swan Yard with PC George Studd on Whit Monday. Having occasion to speak to James Dew, a man much the worse for drink, Double pushed the drunkard off as he appeared as if he was going to topple onto him. Dew fell on the floor. Several men then came out of the taproom and Dew quickly pulled himself up and punched PC Double on the nose followed by another blow which knocked his helmet off. Richard Hubbard, one of the men from the tap room, set about PC Studd with a stick, damaging his helmet, Dew then struck him on his side. Studd drew his staff but was thrown to the ground before he could use it, Hubbard shouting 'Kill the ——' and Studd was kicked in the thigh. Scrambling up, Studd tried to enter the club room but found it locked. A struggle ensued for the staff but the timely intervention of the more sober Mr Clark and Farmer Nelthorpe saw the fracas break up. Hubbard was sentenced to four months' hard labour and Dew to a total of six weeks' imprisonment and an additional fourteen days' hard labour.

12 JUNE   **1381**   The Peasants' Revolt led by John Wrawe in Suffolk breaks out at Liston. By the evening the rebels were at the gates of Bury issuing a proclamation demanding support from the population on pain of decapitation. On the 14th they attacked the abbey, captured and beheaded Sir John Cavendish, the Lord Chief Justice, and later went on to do the same to the Prior of Mildenhall, bringing his head back on a pole for all to see and deride at Bury. Henry Despencer, the warlike Bishop of Norwich, was soon dispatched with his troops and mercenaries and put down the rebels in a bloody engagement (a battle much the same as that at North Walsham where Despencer put down the Peasants' Revolt in Norfolk).

1908 *'The Masked Man' visits Ipswich*. This intriguing and enigmatic character wearing a medieval knight's helmet was on a wager whereby if he was successful in wearing 'the mask' while pushing a pram around the world, and marrying on the way, he would be deemed the winner and collect the veritable fortune of £21,000.

13 June

The 'Masked Man' with one of his support team, 1908.

1883 The death occurred of Edward Fitzgerald (1809–83). Known to the world for his version of the *Rubaiyat* of Omar Khayyam, he spent nearly all his life at Boulge and Woodbridge, and was buried in Boulge churchyard. The rose which grows over his stone was raised at Kew from seed brought by William Simpson, artist, from the grave of Omar Khayyam at Nashapur, and was planted by a few friends in the name of the Omar Khayyam Club on 7 October 1898.

14 June

Edward Fitzgerald's grave in Boulge churchyard, *c.* 1905.

15 JUNE **1881** *The opening of Ipswich's new sewerage system.* The day was a grand occasion with a luncheon held in the new covered reservoir! Before the new system of waste disposal, Cauldwell Brook to the east and the Little Gipping to the west, along with the Cockey that flowed through the town centre, were the sewers of Ipswich. Since at least the fourteenth century each of the waterways had a pit or dunghill near them; a large one below Butter Market was called Colehill while another outside the town walls was called Warwick Pits or was more quaintly known as Colddunghill. Late nineteenth-century excavations revealed the level of Cornhill and Tavern Street had been raised by over 5ft by centuries of compacted dung and debris.

16 JUNE **1920** The execution took place of tram conductor Frederick William Storey (42) by public executioner John Ellis at Ipswich Gaol. Sarah Jane Howard (27) had worked on the trams but had given it up to become housekeeper to Mr Kittle on Camden Road. On 6 February Sarah had gone out for the evening but failed to return. Her battered body was found on the 7th by the railway near some allotments. Investigations were made and it was suggested the father of the baby she was carrying might be Fred Storey. He had certainly been seen in the areas where Sarah was last spotted; he even had an allotment near where her body was discovered. Storey's house was searched and bloody clothes were found. A case was made that Storey simply suffered from bad nosebleeds, hence the stained clothing. The jury at Bury Assizes was not convinced and took just fifteen minutes to find him guilty. Justice Darling donned the black cap and pronounced sentence.

16 JUNE **1787** John Catchpole of Palgrave was a waggoner for most of his life. On reaching the great age of 75, he set out on one last trip to see the sights of London, the scene of his weekly peregrinations as a younger man. Horses and man in need of refreshment, he pulled up at a public house in Sudbury but as the hosteler was removing the horse's bridle it bolted and overturned the cart with John Catchpole still aboard. Terribly bruised, the poor old waggoner died the next day. John was given a fine tombstone in Palgrave churchyard with the epitaph:

> My horses have done running,
> My Waggon is decay'd,
> And now in the Duft my Body is lay'd
> My whip is worn & my work It is done
> And now I'm brought here to my laft home.

Opposite: John Catchpole's ornate tombstone.

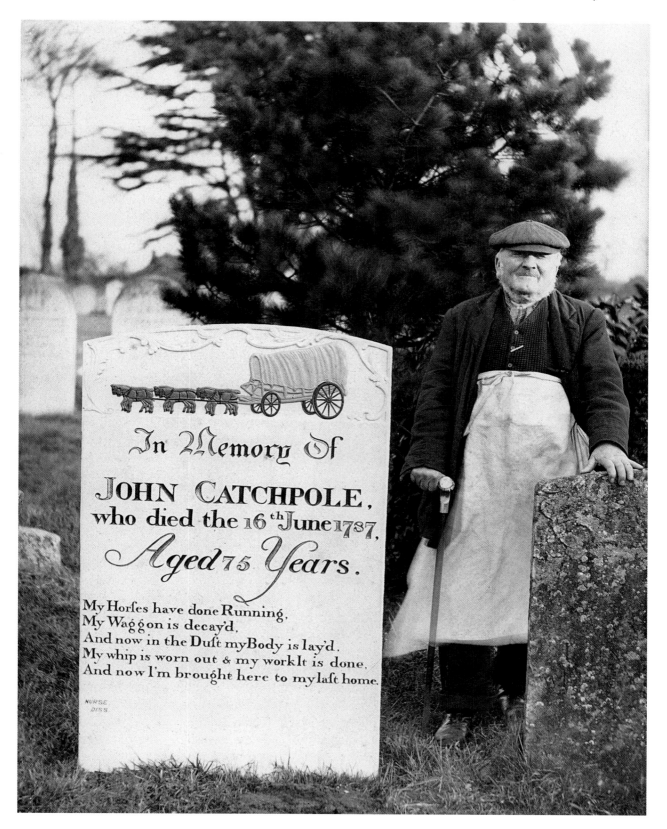

In Memory Of

JOHN CATCHPOLE,
who died the 16th June 1737,
Aged 75 Years.

My Horses have done Running,
My Waggon is decay'd,
And now in the Dust my Body is lay'd.
My whip is worn out & my work It is done,
And now I'm brought here to my last home.

NURSE
DISS

17 June   1917   The last Zeppelin to be shot down on British soil was brought down on land belonging to Holly Tree Farm, Theberton. Forced by engine trouble to fly lower than was safe after an unsuccessful raid on Harwich, the L.48 Zeppelin, under the command of Kapitänleutnant Eichler, was brought down by machine-gun fire from pursuing British aircraft. Only two of the Zeppelin's crew survived the ensuing fireball and the airship fell to the ground. The wreckage was ringed by sentries to prevent souvenir-hunters from taking their pick, and to hold back the crowds who came to see the wreckage. Large pieces of the Zeppelin still exist in museums in Suffolk and around the country; there are even pieces on display in Theberton church. Before their removal to Cannock Chase German Cemetery, those who perished from the crew were buried in the churchyard. A plaque records the RFC chaplain's final words at the original committal, from Romans 14:4: 'Who art thou that judgest another man's servant?'

The burnt-out shell of the Zeppelin at Theberton.

18 June   1874   A savage attack was made by women on a 'blackleg' at Hessett. In the late nineteenth century the notions of farm labourers having unions did not appeal to country landowners and many farmers. Any move towards unions for land workers frequently resulted in 'lockouts' of the workers. In such wars of attrition, where there was no money coming in for food on the labourer's tables, their stance was fiercely defended; often not by the men but their womenfolk. During a prolonged lockout in Suffolk some men would break the strike or turn 'blackleg'. One such character was a Mr Hunt, who went to Hessett to work on a local farm. Waiting until he had finished his day's labour, a crowd of about 100, consisting mostly of womenfolk, turned out to greet him with sneers and jeers. A group of about seven of the women could not contain their anger and struck out at Hunt. The first punch bloodied his nose, another struck the back of his head, while a third pulled him to the ground by his hair, a fourth struck out with her stick, two others put the boot in when he was on the floor and the seventh poured a 'bucket of slop' over him. Each woman appeared before the Bury magistrates and was given the stiff fine of 10s and 4s costs; all were sternly warned that they were lucky not to be gaoled.

1798   The eccentric gentleman William Jennens of Acton Place near Long
Melford died on this day. His will was found, sealed but unsigned, in his coat
pocket. Among his effects were found a chest with bank notes to the amount
of £19,000 and several thousand uncirculated guineas. When his will was
reckoned up it was found he had interests in a vast array of financial
speculations and investments – many of which he had not collected interest
on for over ten years. His total estate amounted to about £800,000 – he was
the equivalent of a multimillionaire in his day.

1911   The execution took place of Arthur Garrod (49) by public executioner
John Ellis at Ipswich Gaol. In a simple and horrible case Garrod and his
girlfriend, Sarah Chilvers (45), were discovered by her son lying on the upper
floor of their Garrett's Buildings home with the room in disarray and their
throats cut. Garrod was apparently still alive. James ran off to summon the
police. PC Painter attended the scene and asked Garrod if he had perpetrated
this deed, to which he replied, 'I have done it. She is dead as a rat, and I wish
I were dead too.' At the trial it transpired that in the heat of a fierce
argument Sarah had started screaming 'Murder!', so he thought he may as
well 'do us both in', first flooring her with a blow from a chopper and then
cutting her throat with his penknife, which he also attempted to use on
himself. The jury found Garrod guilty but urged mercy on the grounds of
provocation. No mercy was shown and the penalty of death was ordered.

Strange and Horrible Tales of Suffolk

The last woman swum for witchcraft in Suffolk. In the course of examining a
pauper at the Angel Inn, Stanningfield, in June 1792, justices Sir Charles
Danvers and Revd John Ord were shocked to hear her accuse another old lady
of being a witch and of having 'disordered her head'. The justices explained
they could take no cognisance of the accusation but, notwithstanding, the
accused lady submitted to the usual ordeal the following Wednesday. At first it
was proposed to weigh her against the church bible, but the local rector
refused to lend the same. Undaunted, the woman's husband, brother and
another man tied a rope around her body and cast her into a horsepond. She
promptly sank, and had to be pulled out in an almost lifeless state. The men,
especially her husband, were rebuked for putting the woman through this
ordeal. He said he thought it better to 'indulge her therein, than to suffer her
destroy herself, which was certain she would have done had she not
undergone the trial'.

1778   Robert Debney (28), son of a local farmer, and William Cooper (18), a
miller's boy, both died on this day at Tunstall. The pair were local smugglers
with a well-concealed underground vault constructed under a heap of horse
manure for their gin contraband. Entombed in their subterranean hole, this
unfortunate pair were fatally overcome by the stench-ridden vapours and
buried in Tunstall churchyard. Part of their epitaph on their newly renovated
stone reads:

Oh think how quickly both these Lives were gone.
Neither Age nor Sickness brought them to the clay;
Death quickly took their strength and Sense away.
Both in the Prime of Life they lost their Breath,
And on a sudden were cast down by death.

23 June

Ipswich prison pillory whipping post and old town stocks.

Old Punishments

Ipswich pillory was erected in Cornhill. It was used for a variety of misdemeanours such as drunkenness and salacious speech and stood as a warning and punishment for dishonest tradesmen and short-changers. The penalty for a first offence was two hours stand; for a second it was eight hours of abuse, rotten fruit, dead animals and excrement being hurled at you.

24 June

1533 The death occurred of Mary Rose Tudor, youngest sister of Henry VIII to live past childhood, and a princess who was to become Queen of France following her marriage to Louis XII. The marriage festivities proved too much for the sickly king and he died three months later. This left the path clear for her to marry her one true love, Charles Brandon, Duke of Suffolk. Her health began to decline rapidly in 1533 and she died on this day. Her body was interred in the Abbey of Bury St Edmunds and moved for safekeeping to St Mary's Church after the abbey was dissolved in 1540. Her peace at St Mary's has not been undisturbed; in 1784 Mary Tudor's coffin was cut open by the churchwardens, her hair torn from her head and sold by the lock!

25 June

Suffolk Old Dame's Leechcraft

Cure for the ague. Go alone to the four crossways at night. Just as the clock strikes twelve turn yourself about three times and drive a tenpenny nail into the ground up to the head, and walk away from the place backwards before the clock has finished striking and you'll miss the ague. But the next person to pass over the nail will take it in your stead.

26 June

1774 John Upson of Woodbridge hanged himself with his own garter after being committed to gaol for felony. The following was found scribbled in a prayer book lying by him.

Farewell, vain world, I've had enough of thee,
And now am Careless what thou say'st of me
Thy smiles I court not, nor thy frowns I fear,
My cares are past, my heart lies easy here.
What faults they find in me take care to shun,
And look at home, enough is to be done.

(Signed) Poor John the Glover

Last Rites

After the decease of John Baret of Bury St Edmunds in 1645, the last wishes of his will were executed to the letter. Two bellmen who went round the town at his death were to have gowns, and to be two of the five torch holders 'for which they were to have twopence and their meat, the sexton receiving twelve pence and his bread, drink and meat'. On his 'thirty-day' the *Requiem Eternam* was to be sounded by means of a chime-barrel ranged over only five notes. At the 'yeerday' the bellmen were to receive fourpence each for going about the town to call on the inhabitants to pray 'for my soule and for my faderis and modrys'.

27 JUNE

1819 On a Southwold gravestone is commemorated the death of David May, son of Henry and Lydia May, who lost his life on board the Ann during an exchange with pirates in the Gulf of Florida. The stone states the following lines 'are inscribed by his widow as the last Melancholy tribute of Affection':

28 JUNE

Not yet have ceas'd to flow a widow's tears
O'er scenes remember'd 'midst the lapse of years.
On foreign seas he fell, but not by storm,
When boisterous winds the heaving waves deform.
Nor the rock beneath the tide concealed.
Nor by the sword which warring natives wield.
But by the foe received in friendship's guise,
By hands of treach'rous pirates lo he dies.
Thou, too art mortal, hast'ning to thy grave
Believe on him whoever lives to save.

1844 The death occurred of John Orridge, Master of Bury Gaol. Just 24 years old when he took over the gaol in 1798, he set about a series of revolutionary measures which became an exemplary model for prisons across the country. Beginning with finding occupations to alleviate prisoner boredom, he did much to improve the security, general health and morals of his prisoners. When the new gaol was constructed

29 JUNE

and opened in December 1805 'at the end of the South Gate' (in an area beside Sicklesmere Road) he did much to argue in favour of prison reformer John Howard's recommendations in its design, as well as suggesting some of his own. His most notable addition was something previously unheard of in prisons: a treadmill. This device allowed a line of prisoners to be kept occupied by treading a 'mill-wheel' of stairs which drove mill stones for grinding corn. Orridge wrote of it, 'The employment afforded by the mill has been found to produce the very best effects both on the health and morals of the prisoners, as well as inducing the habits of industry.' With an improved treadmill installed in 1819, designed and executed by William Cubitt, the notable millwright, treadmills became a feature of many prisons across the country. Orridge died suddenly; he was found dead in his office when he was missed from morning prayers in the prison chapel.

John Orridge.

30 JUNE **1746** Suffolk has a long history of smuggling. One of the most infamous and outstandingly successful bands of smugglers was 'The Hadleigh Gang' who ran hundreds of wagon-loads of contraband goods, especially brandy and tea, into hideouts around the Suffolk countryside. On this night in the parish of Sheverton [sic] about eighty of their number, armed to the teeth with pistols, cutlasses, clubs and daggers ran about 50 hundredweight of 'Tea from parts beyond the sea from which goods customs due to His Majesty'. The only man to be apprehended from the gang after this incident was arrested after a reward of some £500 was offered for any of the gang's capture. He happened to be one of the gang leaders, a John Harvey of Pond Hall near Hadleigh. Witnesses attested to seeing Harvey armed with his brace of pistols helping run the goods ashore and take his share at the end. Found guilty, Harvey was sentenced to seven years' transporatation.

JULY

The Ipswich ducking stool on display at Christchurch Mansion, *c.* 1908.

1 JULY   Strange and Horrible Tales of Suffolk

The belief in lycanthropy, the power invested in some human beings of changing themselves into half man, half wolf creatures was widely believed and feared in medieval and early modern society. A story passed down generations of Lowestoft fisherfolk tells of a wealthy Italian of gentlemanly manners who became fond of a poor fisher boy of about 14 years old. Asked if he would be his page the boy declined, but he did agree to look after the gentleman's dog, a fine curly-coated canine, because the man was going on a long journey. The boy and the dog became inseparable. The boy swam in the sea every morning and the dog took to accompanying him. One day when the boy was about to turn and swim to shore the dog refused and turned on the boy, barking and biting, urging the lad further and further out to sea. As the boy struggled on and was nearing exhaustion he briefly saw the dog's features change – it was none other than the Italian gentleman!

The boy found the last of his energy and managed to reach a fishing smack. Hauling him aboard, the crew saw the terrible scratches and bites from the were-dog all over his neck and shoulders. The dog was seen no more but as the tale circulated local folks recalled a number of boys of like age who had been drowned off Ness Point. A few years earlier the body of a young lad had been washed up on the shore – plainly visible had been the bites and scratches on the throat and shoulders considered to have been caused by a dog.

2 JULY   Old Punishments

In 1477 a crane was erected on the common quay, Ipswich. This device had a secondary purpose to the loading and unloading of cargo; scolds could be suspended from it over the River Orwell and if they really did need cooling down they could be strapped into the ducking stool and dunked in the waters.

3 JULY   1911   *Riot at the Fair*

The Ancient Order of Forresters annual gala at Walsham le Willows was in full swing when an argument broke out about the change given on the steam horses at the travelling fair. Matters became quickly out-of-hand and a group of local men set about trying to wreck the steam horses while some of the fair folk shot at them with rifles from the target stall. Serious shooting broke out when locals fetched their shotguns from their homes. Seven men had received bullet wounds when the landlord of the Anchor at Blo'Norton just happened to be passing the field in his pony and trap and a stray shot caused a fatal wound. Only after this tragic act did order and peace begin to descend on Walsham again. Local folks claim it still rains every year on the anniversary of the riot.

1917 This was the worst night for casualties caused by air raids on Suffolk during the First World War. At 7.30 a.m. eighteen German Gotha Bombers attacked Felixstowe and Harwich. Nine were killed and nineteen were wounded at the Royal Naval Air Service base, where a Curtiss H12 flying boat was also destroyed. On the 22nd the Gotha Squadron carried out a second attack, killing thirteen and injuring twenty-six. Most of the casualties in this raid were suffered by members of the Suffolk Regiment at a local army base.

4 JULY

Last Rites

At Woodbridge the burial feast was called 'mulled-ale', and the dying person would have chosen what the bearers would have to drink. The bearers all had a drink before they went to church, while the mourners drank afterwards. The mourners (even those not known for their religious observance) would not fail to attend church the following Sunday when tradition held that the clergyman was obliged to preach a sermon from any text the mourners chose.

5 JULY

Strange and Horrible Tales of Suffolk

In his *Doome Warning*, published in 1582, Stephen Bateman relates that 'Fishers toke a disfigured divell, in a certain Stoure [possibly the estuary of the River Stour]. A horrible monster with a goat's head, and eyes shyning like fyre, whereupon they were all afrayde and ranne awaye; and that the ghoste plunged himself under the ice, and running uppe and downe in the Stoure made a terrible noyse and sound.'

6 JULY

A section of the Wenhaston 'Doom'.

County Bridewells and Gaols visited by Prison Reformer John Howard

Clare Bridewell was visited on four occasions between 1776 and 1782. On most visits there was only one prisoner except in April 1779 when there were three prisoners and two impressed men.

7 JULY

Howard described the prison as consisting of a workroom, two lodging rooms with boarded bedsteads; he notes: 'The work room close glazed, and made offensive by a closet in it . . . Prisoners have no access to the well of fine water'. The prison was thatched and the walls made of clay with the exception of the men's lodging room which was boarded, there was no courtyard 'and the whole of it ruinous.' Howard makes special note that 'the prisoner in 1776, a woman, at work, in irons . . . each prisoner pays a penny a day for straw etc.' The keeper was a weaver with a salary of £13 13s 4d. Howard's closing observations were: 'At my first visit in 1779, the three prisoners, though they were women, had each a heavy chain, and the two impressed men had chains and logs. No justices have visited this prison for many years.'

8 JULY **1899** *The Wortham murder.* Mrs Eliza Dixon of Wortham Long Green was fetching some stout for supper from the Dolphin Inn. Inside the crowded pub playing ten pins was local labourer George Nunn (18) who insisted on buying her a drink. She bought her quart of stout and set back home about 10 p.m., Nunn left shortly afterwards. When she did not arrive home by 11 p.m. Eliza's husband, James, set off for the Dolphin and made enquiries. He was soon at the Nunn residence but all were in bed and when George was roused he claimed only to have seen Eliza in the pub. PC Mills of Palgrave was summoned and a search organised. At about 2.30 a.m. a woman's body was found in a dry watercourse close to the road across the green. She had been repeatedly stabbed and her throat was cut. Supt Page from Eye was summoned and a murder investigation opened. The body was soon identified as that of Eliza Dixon. When questioned, Nunn was found to have blood stains on his hands and clothes and was arrested. Urged by his father to confess, Nunn stated he had attempted to pay for an indecent act with Eliza and a row ensued where he pushed her to the ground, kicked her and stabbed her in the throat with his knife. Conveyed initially to Eye lock-up he was transferred to Ipswich Gaol to await trial and appeared before the Suffolk Assizes at Bury. In an open-and-shut case Nunn was found guilty and sentenced to death. George Nunn was executed inside Ipswich Gaol on Tuesday 21 November 1899. A crowd of mostly workmen and boys still assembled on Bond Street to watch the Black Flag raised as a sign that the execution had been carried out. When the flag was raised, up went the cry 'There it goes', after which the crowd quietly dispersed.

9 JULY **1876** A traction engine which had been undergoing repairs at Cornish's foundry on Risbygate Street was being removed through the town. When passing down Loom's Lane its chain snapped and all control was lost of the engine which soon picked up tremendous speed, smashing off the corner of a baker's shop at the turn into Northgate Street and dashing into a house on the opposite side, tearing down the studwork in the lower rooms. Fortunately no one was hurt and there was no cellar, otherwise the engine would probably have smashed through and set the building alight. It was some hours before the chain could be repaired and the engine backed out, by which time some hundreds of people had gathered at the scene of this singular accident.

EAST SUFFOLK CONSTABULARY.

HABITUAL DRUNKARDS—LICENSING ACT, 1902.

The attention of licensed persons and secretaries of clubs registered under Part III. of the Licensing Act, 1902, is hereby called to the provisions of Sections 6 of that Act, which applies to persons convicted as habitual drunkards, and notified as such to police authorities.

"(a) If the convicted person within three years after the date of the conviction purchases or obtains, or attempts to purchase or obtain any intoxicating liquor at any premises licensed for the sale of intoxicating liquor by retail, or at the premises of any club registered in pursuance of the provisions of Part III. of this Act, he shall be liable, on summary conviction, to a fine not exceeding, for the first offence, twenty shillings, and for any subsequent offence, forty shillings; and

(b) If the holder of any licence authorising the sale of intoxicating liquor by retail whether for consumption on or off the premises, or any person selling, supplying, or distributing intoxicating liquor, or authorising such sale, supply, or distribution on the premises of a club registered in conformity with the provisions of Part III. of this Act, within that period knowingly sells, supplies, or distributes, or allows any person to sell, supply, or distribute intoxicating liquor to, or for the consumption of, any such person, he shall be liable on summary conviction, for the first offence, to a fine not exceeding ten pounds, and for any subsequent offence in respect of the same person, to a fine not exceeding twenty pounds."

In accordance with the regulations made by the Police Authority for the Administrative County of East Suffolk under the above-mentioned Act and Section, notice is hereby given that the following person has been declared to be a habitual drunkard under the Act 61 and 62 Vict., c. 60, and that the provisions of the Licensing Act, 1902 (Section 6) as above quoted now apply to such person.

PORTRAIT AND DESCRIPTION OF HABITUAL DRUNKARD.　　No. 2.

Name. ELLEN MARIA MOORE, known as " Nellie."

Residence Sun Lane, Woodbridge.

Place of business, or where employed. None fixed.

Age. 31. Height 5 ft. 1 in.

Build. Stout.

Hair. Dark brown.

Eyes. Blue.

Complexion. Fresh.

Shape of Nose. Slightly Roman.

Shape of Face. Full

Peculiarities or marks. Small scar centre of forehead, mole right cheek.

Profession or occupation. Married woman.

Date and nature of conviction. 17th March, 1904. Disorderly and drunk. One month's imprisonment with hard labour, and notice of the conviction ordered to be sent to the Police Authority for East Suffolk.

Court at which convicted. Petty Sessions for the Petty Sessional Division of Woodbridge.

Date of expiration of this notice, 16th March, 1907.

Should any known habitual drunkard attempt to purchase or obtain any intoxicating liquor at any premises licensed for the sale of intoxicating liquor by retail, or at the premises of any registered club, it is requested that the person refusing to supply the liquor will, as soon as practicable, give information of such attempt to the Police of the district.

JASPER G. MAYNE, CAPTAIN,

COUNTY HALL, IPSWICH. ●

Chief Constable of East Suffolk.

26TH MARCH, 1904.

10 JULY **1913** *Murder and suicide at Lowestoft.* Animosity between Louis Thain and his wife Fanny had built up over the years since they married. Thain had charmed and married the appealing Fanny on a handful of lies. Fanny was well provided for in the terms of her dear departed's will but she would lose a third if she married again. Thain claimed he was a wealthy merchant and could make up any shortfalls. Once they were married it soon became apparent there was no such wealth. As time went on he drank and whittled away what money she had left until matters came to a head in July 1913. Following a violent exchange Fanny moved in with friends and set about divorcing Thain. The court hearing was set for the morning of 13 July but Thain did not show, going instead to Yarmouth to buy a revolver. In the afternoon he swaggered into the courtroom, where the evidence for a separation was made clear and was granted. Thain stormed out of the court. Fanny and her friends were making their way home from the court when Thain confronted them in Junction Passage. Raising his gun he shot at Fanny but the bullet wounded one of her friends, another friend stepped in and told Fanny to run but Thain fired again and killed Fanny. Local people came out to investigate and a Mr Myhill ended up being shot too. Deciding the situation was hopeless, Thain beat the gallows by taking matters into his own hands and blew his own brains out with his revolver.

11 JULY **1745** 'Giffling' Jack Corbolt, a respectable Yarmouth innkeeper by day and violent smuggler by night, with his team of fifty smugglers, ran a massive cargo of tea and brandy ashore at Benacre Warren. Customs authorities estimated that by this time 4,500 horse-loads of contraband had been run across the Suffolk beaches since the start of the year and action had to be taken. After dogged pursuits and many abortive traps, the excise men eventually captured Giffling Jack and some of his cronies. Held in secure cells, he had to be transported to Norwich for trial. A team of experienced riding officers were charged with the duty but were outnumbered and outgunned by a twenty-man ambush. Giffling Jack escaped into the night again.

12 JULY **1876** John Taylor (66), a thatcher who resided at Debenham, was a well-known drunkard who argued with his wife Maria regularly. Raising his gun to within inches of her head, he fired. The shot shattered Maria's bonnet but she remained physically unharmed. No doubt believing he had killed her, Taylor retreated to his cottage and barricaded himself in. The situation became a siege, with Taylor threatening instant death to anyone who dared to enter. A report in the *Norfolk & Suffolk Journal* explored the expedients suggested to extricate him: 'one thought the fire engine would dislodge him, for as a devoted worshipper of Bacchus he had a mortal hatred of pure water'. Another suggested smoking him out by burning brimstone; but one who knew him well suggested beer. Beer aplenty was got to Taylor until he was so drunk an entry was forced and through his totally smashed house Taylor was retrieved and arrested. On leaving the house Taylor received a true rogue's march to the lock-up as villagers lined the way, each with a kick, punch or scratch for him. Brought before the assizes, he was found guilty of attempted murder and sentenced to penal servitude for life.

1905 *Lowestoft bride murdered.* Charles Hartley Taylor (22), a native of York, was married to pretty Miss Norah G. Saul (19), daughter of Robert Saul of 7 Commercial Road, Lowestoft at the Register Office. Hiring rooms at 108 Russell Street, Peterborough 'a more loving couple never started upon their honeymoon'. All seemed very well until 4.30 a.m. on 13 July, Mr and Mrs Humphrey, the landlord and lady at the boarding house, heard four pistol shots fired, with a few seconds between each shot. Running to their guests' room, the only response they had was a gurgling noise. Shouldering the door, Mr Humphrey found it had been barricaded but forcing through he entered the room. 'Mrs Taylor was lying with her back to her husband with a bullet wound in the back of her neck, and he was lying on his back with a revolver in his right hand and blood pouring from his mouth saturating the bed, with its dainty hangings of pale blue and red.' After the police had been summoned, Mrs Taylor was soon removed to an infirmary, Taylor himself was already dead. Upon investigation it was found that she had been shot three times while she was asleep, then Taylor had put the little American seven-chambered double-action revolver in his mouth and pulled the trigger. The reason why Taylor perpetrated this terrible act remains a mystery.

13 JULY

1871 A report appeared in the *Diss Express* of a case heard at Hartismere Petty Sessions of 'indecent behaviour in church'. PC Higginson reported complaints from the vicar and churchwardens about the behaviour of Emma Stammers, Lucy Girling and Charlotte Jackaman, all of Mendlesham. Apparently the young ladies had 'kept flinging flowers about and endeavoured to attract the attention of some of the young men . . . their conversation could be heard all over the church. Unfortunately the chair of the bench hearing the case happened to be a clergyman – the Revd Thomas Lee French – who felt strongly enough to describe the girls' behaviour as 'disgraceful', and he marked his disgust with a heavy fine of 4 or 5s for each girl and 5s costs – or seven days' imprisonment each.

14 JULY

1592 An inquest was held into the death of William Reade of Ballingdon. Felled by the staff of Thomas Throughton, a local yeoman, whose defence was that while 'flourishinge with his staff' (stated as being worth four pennies) it struck a post and shot from his hand. It felled William Reade with a mortal blow to the right side of his forehead, a wound from which he died later that day. To the amazement of Thomas Dogwood, the coroner, the jury believed the tale and returned a verdict of 'not guilty by misfortune'.

15 JULY

Last Rites

In 1885 the *East Suffolk Almanac* reported an 'Excessive Display of Mourning'. When the mourners returned home Mr Grant tied crêpe upon all window shutters, to show how deeply he mourned; and as Fisher knew that his grief for Mrs Fisher was deeper, he not only decorated his shutters, but he fixed 5 yards of black bombazine on the bell-pull and dressed his whole family in mourning. Then Grant determined that his duty to the departed was not to let himself be beaten by a man who couldn't feel any genuine sorrow, so he sewes a black flag on his lightning rod, and festooned the front of his house

16 JULY

with black alpaca. Then Fisher became excited, and he expressed his sense of bereavement by painting his dwelling black, and by putting up a monument to Mrs Fisher in his front yard. Grant thereupon stained his yellow horse with lampblack, tied crêpe to his cow's horn, daubed his dog with ink and began to wipe his nose with a black handkerchief.

17 JULY   **1888**   The case was reported of George Wilfred Frederick Ellis (35) at Suffolk Winter Assizes held at Bury. Ellis was appointed curate at Wetheringsett in 1883. A popular priest with the locals, he performed baptisms, marriages, funerals and regular services in the village until by chance he was found out and exposed as a fraud impersonating a priest. Ellis's paperwork proved to be forged and he was apprehended by Inspector Bly of Eye in March 1888. In a trial where no less a luminary than the Lord Bishop of Norwich gave evidence, the jury were left in no doubt of the answers given on oath and returned a verdict of 'guilty' without leaving their box. Ellis was sentenced to seven years' penal servitude in Dartmoor prison. The matter did, however, leave a legacy behind in the village. Where did the people stand who had been married by Ellis over the five years of his tenure? Were they still married or not, and did this make their children bastards? A special Act of Parliament had to be drawn up recognising all of Ellis's marriages 'as valid as if the same had been solemnised before a duly ordained clergyman of the Church of England'.

18 JULY   **Strange and Horrible Tales of Suffolk**
Suffolk has been subject to visitations of Black Plague since the fourteenth century. Lowestoft suffered plagues in 1349, 1547, 1579, 1585 and 1603. In 1603, 316 of Lowestoft's inhabitants fell victim to the contagion. Ipswich also suffered dreadfully in 1603. In 1636 plague raged at Bury St Edmunds, and so depopulated was the town that grass grew in the street. Four hundred families lay sick at the same time and were maintained at the public charge which is said to have amounted to £200 a week. In 1666 the plague came to Woodbridge and carried off the minister, his wife and child, as well as 300 townsfolk. Needham Market was a flourishing market town until the plague came there in 1665. Chains were put across the entrance roads of the town to the east and west in efforts to contain the disease. Food was exchanged at these points for money 'cleansed' in a vinegar and water mixture. The last outbreak of Black Plague in Britain is also recorded as having occurred in Suffolk, having been brought into the village of Chelmondiston via the tiny quay at Pin Mill in 1918.

The Butt & Oyster
Inn beside the bay at
Pin Mill, *c.* 1905.

1825   A report appeared in *The Times* of a man being swum to discover if he was a 'wizard' at Wickham Skeith. The man in question was a wizened 67-year-old huckster named Isaac Stebbings. Near him lived a weaver whose wife suffered some form of undiagnosed mental illness. A nearby farmer also suffered the same affliction. Malicious tongues with nothing better to do began to wag, and when Stebbings was seen to pass the local cobbler's window a number of times and the cobbler's wax failed to mix, it was the final straw and 'conclusive proof' Stebbings had 'the evil eye'. Combined with a few other strange coincidences or concoctions of the imagination, the situation was taken into control by Stebbings himself who offered to be swum as a witch at

19 JULY

A different type of
ducking – baptisms
in the village pond at
Foxford, *c.* 1910.

Grimmer Pond on Wickham Green the following Saturday at 2 p.m. Escorted by villagers and many from the surrounding settlements to the pond on the appointed day, he stepped into the water with four male witnesses and with the parish constable on the banks to keep order. When chest-high in water, the four men lifted him onto his back and there he floated for ten minutes – much to the frustration of the crowd. Someone shouted, 'Give him another', and the process was repeated. The crowd wanted a dunking and shouted, 'Try him again and dip him under.' One of the men in the water put his foot on Stebbings' chest only to have his feet come up as he went under. These trials saw poor old Stebbings in the water for almost an hour and totally exhausted. The crowd were still not satisfied and wanted another test carried out the following week with another man of similar size and age to be 'swum' next to him; this was planned for the following weekend. The local clergy and churchwardens would have no more of this abomination and the following week when the crowds drew up they were sent away by the clerics!

20 JULY   **1876**   The capture was announced of Samuel Wright, a mat-maker of Glemsford who had been on the run from Bury prison for several months. Recaptured at Fulham Gardens in London by a London detective and Inspector Keeble of Bury police, Wright had evaded capture so effectively because 'his movements and appearance were of such a common place character'. The report concludes, 'Wright is back again in his old quarters.'

21 JULY   **1897**   It had been a year of severe snow, storms and rain and on this day tempest and torrent struck Ipswich. Streets were rapidly flooded and two boys were killed by a lightning strike.

22 JULY   **Strange and Horrible Tales of Suffolk**
Spontaneous human combustion? The last of the Ipswich witches, one Grace Pett, met her end in 1744. Allegedly, she laid her curse on a local farmer's sheep. Superstition held that redress against the witch could be obtained by fastening the poor sheep to the ground, burying its feet in the earth, and burning the rest of the beast. The following morning Grace Pett's body was found lying on the floor near her hearth. She had been burnt to a cinder – except her hands and feet! But the boarded floor, on which she lay, was not even scorched.

23 JULY   **1844**   In mid-nineteenth-century Suffolk, strong-arm tactics were maintained against any of those who would transgress the laws of person or property. Man-traps and spring-guns were still known on country estates, and high walls with spikes and broken glass on top were common. At Suffolk Assizes the stance of the judiciary was well evinced on this day when Robert Grimwade (29) of Polstead was sentenced to ten years' transportation for sending a letter threatening to burn down the property of three local landowners. Grimwade had followed Faber Copsey (19) of Glemham who was transported for life for firing a barn and William Gill of Drinkstone who received the same for setting fire to a stack of barley; both of them were sentenced at the previous March Assizes.

ESTABLISHED 1840.

FRANK FREWER,
MARBLE, GRANITE & STONE
MONUMENTAL WORKS,
21, CEMETERY ROAD,
IPSWICH.

Imperishable Lead Letters in Marble or Stone.

Estimates given for all descriptions of Cemetery and General Masonry.

Advert for Frewer's Monumental Works, 1885.

24 JULY   1834   James Leggett (16) died on this day. The epitaph on his grave recorded:

> I drove a Roan, the Horse was young,
> To manage him I tried.
> A Bramble across my path; I fell;
> The wheels, they pressed my side.
> Then bid farewell to all my friends and fears
> Now wipe away your streaming tears.
> Great were my sufferings time I remained,
> But the Lord soon eased me of my pain.

25 JULY   1815   Elizabeth Woolterton (49), a widow of North Cove, was executed for murder before a large crowd at Ipswich Gaol.

26 JULY   1648   Richard Evered was laid in his early grave at Long Melford on this day. As the Civil War was drawing to a close the counties of Norfolk and Suffolk had seen little serious military action. Most had gone with Cromwell and Royalist sympathisers were forced to comply or went with the flow, holding their tongues on the matter. Drink can have a nasty way of twisting banter and sporting talk into violence and when young Richard Evered, son of a wealthy local clothier family, had his tongue loosened into a political argument with Parliamentarian Roger Green at the Bull Inn he thought it best to retire to the front hall and leave the matter be. Sadly the fiery temperament of Green could not be quenched without bloodshed and he stabbed Evered with his dagger, killing him instantly. The Parliamentary Coroner's Court found Green guilty of murder but no record of his execution can be found.

27 JULY   1847   At Suffolk Summer Assizes, Edward Coots (15), a labourer from Framlingham, was charged with having burglariously broken into and entered the house of John Oakley at Framlingham. Accused of stealing a tea chest, two silver caddy spoons and a variety of other articles, he was found guilty and, because it was not his first offence, he was given ten years' transportation. At the same assize, Ipswich labourer George Barker (27) was found guilty of the wilful murder of Elizabeth Jager in the parish of St Margaret in Ipswich. His sentence? Twenty years' transportation!

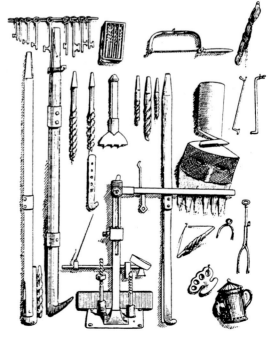

Burglars' tools.

Off to Bury Fair, 1770.

1835 The old Bury Fair had gradually turned into a bawdy, boozy and **28 JULY** noisesome festival since its original establishment in 1272. By the nineteenth century the sensibilities of the time wanted to tone down and even abolish the fair. Tempers flared at the fair in 1834 when Mr King, an Ipswich publican, erected a large dancing booth. Messrs Boldero and Mower set about pulling it down and were stopped neither by the local constable nor alderman. King took all to court on this date and the bench found in his favour awarding £5 damages.

1791 In the rural communities of the past, things which may seem trivial to **29 JULY** modern sensibilities were viewed very differently. Roger Benstead was a popular local farmer and a real family man, but a series of petty disputes with neighbouring farmer Thomas Briggs were brought to a head by the persistence of Briggs in encouraging his cows onto Benstead's pastures. Following legal wrangles and idiosyncrasies of the law which seemed to infuriate and frustrate Benstead he could see no other means to end the problem than to remove Briggs – permanently. He was driven to stoop low enough to manipulate and threaten Thomas Harper, his apprentice lad, to shoot Briggs on this day. The shot did not prove fatal but Briggs died from loss of blood as he attempted to drag himself home. Benstead, his son and Harper were all arrested and accused of murder. The truth of the case soon emerged and only farmer Benstead was found guilty of the murder at Bury Lent

Assizes in 1792. After execution his body was removed to Undley Common near his Lakenheath farm and hung from a gibbet as a warning to others.

30 JULY **1584** 'Old ladie Ichingham' was buried in Barsham churchyard, having died after reputedly attaining the age of 110 years.

31 JULY **1809** Matthew Riley (27) and John Dogarty (22) both of Ipswich, were executed for murder, side-by-side on the gallows trap, in front of a huge crowd at the County Gaol, Ipswich.

Lowestoft Cemetery Chapel House.

AUGUST

The door that still bears the claw marks from the visit of the Black Dog to
Blythburgh Church in 1577.

1 AUGUST **1672** *Lammas Day.* Magdalen Holyday (18), maidservant to Simon Jones, parson of Saxmundham, was 'possessed by spell of a witch'. On this day while serving the parson and his family their midday meal of dumplings, the poor girl uttered a loud shriek and complained of a large pin in the upper part of her leg. On examination she could feel the pin under her skin but no point of entry could be discerned. The pain having continued for some time, two apothecaries were sent for. Despite making an incision to remove the pin, none could be found. The maid stated a few days before that an old woman had come to the door and begged a pin; the maid stated she had none to give but the old woman went away muttering something. Until the pain began she thought nothing more of the incident. As the days passed the pain did not abate and her fitful sleep was troubled by 'wicked apparitions'. More surgeons came to her aid and 'anointed the part' for three weeks with the following embrocation: dog's grease, well mixed, four ounces; bear's fat, two ounces; eight ounces of Capon's grease; four and twenty slips of mistletoe, cut in pieces and powdered small with gum of turpentine, put close into a phial till it formed into green balsam. Over the three weeks the poor girl is stated to have vomited some of the following substances: paring of nails, crooked pins, bodkins, lumps of red hair, one thousand two hundred worms, pieces of glass and 'great bones like teeth of a horse'. When all hope was given up she brought up with violent retching 'a whole row of pins stuck on blew paper', after which the girl made a full recovery and eventually grew to womanhood, marrying a steward to Sir John Heveningham to whom she bore four healthy children.

2 AUGUST **1848** Hannah Bowyer appeared at the assizes, held at Ipswich, charged with the murder of her 3-year-old illegitimate daughter, Beatrice. Her lover, William Glasscock, did not want 'the sickly child' and was pressurising her to 'get rid of it'. He meant to put the child in a home or farm her out to relatives; he did not mean kill her or, more likely, his conscience pricked him and, fearing the gallows when the child died, he blamed Hannah. At the inquest Charles Adderton, the keeper of the Cock Inn at Clare, stated he observed Hannah boiling up hemlock, but Glasscock told her it was sheep's parsley, and gave the child about half a cup. The post-mortem revealed no trace of poison and thus the inquest jury could return no other verdict than death by unknown causes. Hannah's case still proceeded to the assizes. All evidence was purely circumstantial and, with no obvious foul cause of death, Hannah was found 'not guilty'.

3 AUGUST **1876** The Bravo case or Balham mystery had the country engrossed. The case revolved around the poisoning of barrister Charles Bravo (30). Suspicion fell on his wife Florence (25), but the case was never solved. As ever, the local press sought local connections to national events and the Suffolk newspapers were full of the actions of Mrs Jane Cannon Cox, Florence's friend and at whose house the Bravos were guests when the alleged poisoning took place. Mrs Cox was proved to have had a sojourn at Woodbridge in 1869 when she resided at Holly Lodge and advertised in the *Ipswich Journal* as having a limited number of places for young ladies desiring 'a superior education combined with every comfort and refinement of a well-appointed home'. Her school did not take off and she left after a few months. Making the acquaintance of many local well-to-do families, she was remembered as 'being accompanied by a mulatto female servant who went by the name of Bravo'.

1577 *Devil dogs in Suffolk.* Probably the most infamous of all grim Suffolk tales is that of the Black Dog (or Dogs) which paid visitations to church congregations at Bungay and Blythburgh on this day. According to the contemporary account of *A Strange and Terrible Wunder wrought very late in the parish church of Bungay* the town was in the grip of a great storm of pouring rain, thunder and lightning whereby the rumbles were thought to

4 AUGUST

shake the church itself. The already fearful congregation was plunged into blind terror as a 'black dog, or the divel in such likeness [was seen], running along the body of the church with such great swiftness, and incredible haste among people, in a visible form and shape, passed between two persons, as they were kneeling upon their knees, and occupied in prayer as it seemed, wrung the necks of them bothe at one instant clene backward . . . [that they] stragely dyed . . . Passing by an other man of the congregation in the church, gave him such a gripe on the back, that therewith all he was presently drawn togither and shrunk up, as it were a piece of lether scorched in a hot fire; or as the mouth of a purse or bag drawen together with a string. The man, albeit hee was in so strange a taking, dyed not, but as it is thought yet alive.' Meanwhile, outside the church, the clerk, clearing a gutter, was thrown to the ground by one almighty clap of thunder, possibly as the dog left the church. Apart from the fall, the clerk received no other injury but the poor church clock was 'wrung in sunder and broken in peces'.

It is then possible this same hideous devil dog proceeded to Blythburgh, where with an almighty clap of thunder the steeple fell in and smashed the font; then 'the like thing entred, in the same shape and similitude', placed himself on a beam and swung into the church where he 'slew two men and a lad & burned the hand of another person

Blythburgh Church.

that was there among the rest of the company, of whom divers were blasted. This mischief thus wrought, he flew with wonderful force to no little feare of the assembly out of the church in a hideous and hellish likenes.' Although no marks of the devil dog's visit remain in Bungay church, he is remembered on the town coat of arms, while at Blythburgh, deep scorch marks are still visible on the church door; some say they are from ball-lightning while others still maintain they are the lasting scratch marks left behind by its most unwanted visitor.

1842 *Ipswich Borough Police dismissed.* The Ipswich police was brought into existence on 1 March 1836. After almost ten years of good police work with the loss of two good superintendents to the East Suffolk force in 1841 and early 1842, the Ipswich Borough Police went into sharp decline. Disciplinary offences became rife. The police barrack block was situated near St Mary le Tower church. The premises were an old workhouse that housed both married and single men. Complaints of disorderly conduct came thick and fast on Sundays from members of the church congregation who observed our upstanding law officers drinking and 'using improper language'. Women in single men's quarters were also noted! The force was described as being in 'a deplorable state of affairs', so the Ipswich Watch Committee undertook drastic measures and dismissed the entire establishment.

WEST SUFFOLK CONSTABULARY

THE FOLLOWING MAXIMS

Are to be strictly observed and borne in mind by the Constables of the Force

1. Constables are placed in authority to PROTECT, not to OPPRESS, the PUBLIC.
2. To do which effectually, they must earnestly and systematically exert themselves to PREVENT CRIME.
3. When a Crime has been committed, no time should be lost, nor exertions spared, to discover and bring to justice the OFFENDERS.
4. Obtain a knowledge of all REPUTED THIEVES, and IDLE and DISORDERLY PERSONS.
5. Watch narrowly all Persons having NO VISIBLE MEANS OF SUBSISTENCE.
6. Prevent VAGRANCY.
7. Be IMPARTIAL in the discharge of duties.
8. Discard from the mind all POLITICAL and SECTARIAN prejudices.
9. Be COOL and INTREPID in the discharge of duties in emergencies and unavoidable conflicts.
10. Avoid ALTERCATIONS, and display PERFECT COMMAND of TEMPER under INSULT and gross PROVOCATION, to which all Constables must occasionally be liable.
11. NEVER STRIKE but in SELF-DEFENCE, nor treat a Prisoner with more Rigour than may be absolutely necessary to prevent escape.
12. Practice the most complete SOBRIETY, one instance of DRUNKENNESS will render a Constable liable to DISMISSAL.
13. Treat with the utmost CIVILITY all classes of HER MAJESTY'S SUBJECTS, and cheerfully render ASSISTANCE to all in need of it.
14. Exhibit DEFERENCE and RESPECT to the MAGISTRACY.
15. Promptly and cheerfully OBEY all SUPERIOR OFFICERS.
16. Render an HONEST, FAITHFUL, and SPEEDY account of all MONIES and PROPERTY, whether intrusted with them for others, or taken possession of in the execution of duty.
17. With reference to the foregoing, bear especially in mind that "HONESTY IS THE BEST POLICY."
18. Be perfectly neat and clean in Person and Attire.
19. Never sit down in a PUBLIC HOUSE or BEER SHOP.
20. **AVOID TIPPLING.**
21. It is the interest of every man to devote some portion of his spare time to the practice of READING and WRITING and the general improvement of his mind.
22. IGNORANCE is an insuperable bar to promotion.

G D GRIFFITHS
Chief Constable

Guidance for West Suffolk police constables, *c.* 1845.

6 August   **1876**   George Barnaby (26) known as 'The Suffolk Jack Sheppard', had been indicted for setting fire to a vessel called *The Maryland* at Southwold on 3 April and appeared at the Suffolk Assizes. Answering for this offence as well as for an assault on the night watchman at Ipswich Gaol, and asking for another felony to be taken into consideration, Barnaby was sentenced to ten years' penal servitude.

7 August   **1876**   Reports appeared of the sad case of a man named Bradd who committed suicide at Newmarket 'by nearly severing his head from his body with a razor'. Married only a couple of months before, Bradd was the driver of the omnibus between Wickhambrook and Newmarket when a cricketer was killed by falling while endeavouring to get on the bus. There was no way this accident was the fault of Bradd but before his suicide Bradd was 'impressed with the idea that he was to blame and had taken to drinking'.

8 August   **1812**   *The execution of Daniel Dawson.* Dawson was a tout who lodged on Newmarket High Street. Persuaded by two villainous bookies named Bland to prevent some heavily backed horses owned by Richard Prince from running, he enlisted the help of 'a ramshackle old chemist named Bishop'. Learning how to dissolve arsenic in water he mixed some of the poison in Prince's horse trough. Dawson always swore he did not intend to kill the horses but simply to slow them down or make them temporarily ill. After Prince received some intimation of the poisoning attempt he did not permit use of the trough but by the following day Prince decided the poisoning attempt was 'all gammon' and decided to let the horses drink from there. In the meantime Dawson thought the arsenic was too weak and had visited again to 'hot up' the potency of the poison by adding more! Some of the horses knew something was amiss and would not drink, some drank a little and were seized by violent griping. The horses of Sir Sitwell Sitwell were dosed with castor oil and recovered but tragically the order for Sir Frank Standish's horses was to wait for Dr Bowles of Cambridge. This delay proved fatal and the horses died in agony. The Jockey Club instantly put up posters offering a 500-guinea reward for information. Evidence was soon gathered against Dawson and he was sent to Cambridge Assizes. Bishop turned King's evidence and sealed Dawson's fate. Before execution Dawson admitted poisoning horses at Doncaster a couple of years previously. A scaffold was specially erected on top of Cambridge Castle and Dawson was hanged before a crowd of 15,000 spectators.

9 August   **1780**   At a time when French and American privateers stalked the waters off eastern England even humble fishermen and their boats were in danger. A cod smack sailing off Southwold was pursued by what was believed to be a heavily armed smuggling vessel. The fishermen were saved when the pursuing ship was forced to flee when a fleet of colliers hoved into view. This aggressive smuggling ship transpired to be a 150-ton American privateer named *Fearnought*. Armed with eighteen four-pounder cannon the ship was under the command of notorious pirate Daniel Fall, who terrorised the east coast until he was finally chased away by HMS *Albermarle* under the command of no less a man than Horatio Nelson!

1854   The Parochial School at Capel St Mary was struck by lightning, killing three children. Gripped by a terrific storm between two and three in the afternoon the eighty-odd children attending school that day were receiving lessons in their classrooms when lightning struck the western gable of the school splitting it in half and dashing in the windows, one of which smashed into the boys' classroom, filling it with flames and dust. The lightening then ran across the ceiling and set the thatched roof on fire. Children lay all over the floor screaming and crying piteously. Seeing the fire villagers ran to the scene and most children were evacuated to safety but the dead bodies of three little boys clearly showing the marks of lightning strike were removed to a nearby hovel. At the inquest it was plain the boys had died instantly and a verdict of 'Accidental death by being struck by lightning' was returned. It was said the schoolmaster, Mr Alexander prematurely aged after the disaster and was never the same again.

10 AUGUST

The Parochial School at Capel St Mary after the lightning strike of 10 August 1854.

1828 The execution took place of William Corder, 'The Red Barn Murderer' in front of Bury St Edmunds prison by James Foxton the executioner from London's Newgate Prison. William Corder was the son of a prosperous Polstead farmer but he did not appear to have inherited much of his father's business sense. Having gone to London he returned penniless in 1826 and shortly after started a relationship with Maria Marten. She was no shrinking violet; she had had more than one lover and at least one illegitimate child before she met him. In 1827 she gave birth at the rooms she shared with Corder at Sudbury. This male child apparently died soon after Maria's return to Polstead and was buried, and remains undiscovered, in the village. On 18 May 1827 Corder told Maria to make discreet preparations to travel to Ipswich where they would be married. She was to meet him in the evening at the Red Barn disguised as a man and they would elope.

What happened next we cannot be sure of, but Maria was never seen alive again. Corder reappeared at Polstead a few days later stating he had left Maria at Ipswich and then he departed to London where he began advertising for a wife and soon set up a school with Mary Moore, his new (or first) bride, in Brentford. What happened next caused a sensation. Maria's mother dreamt her daughter was dead and buried under the dirt floor of the Red Barn. Persuading her mole-catcher husband to investigate, old Mr Marten took his mole spade and investigated. His wife's dream proved horribly true and the body of Maria was unearthed on 19 April 1828. She had been shot and apparently stabbed. Corder was traced and brought back for trial. He claimed she had shot herself and vehemently denied stabbing her. The witnesses and evidence, however, piled up against him, he was found guilty and sentenced to death.

Governor Orridge at the gaol implored Corder to confess, to which he acceded with the words 'I am a guilty man' and produced a written confession that he signed on the morning of his execution (although Corder

GOD'S
REVENGE AGAINST MURDER.

"WHOSO SHEDDETH MAN'S BLOOD, BY MAN SHALL HIS BLOOD BE SHED."

No. 6.　　　　　SATURDAY, JUNE 1, 1833.　　　　　PRICE ONE PENNY.

Corder burying the Body of Maria Marten.

The Arrest of Corder.

always maintained he did not stab Maria – perhaps her father's small mole spade, driven into the ground while searching for her, caused her wounds). From as early as 5 a.m. the crowd of gentry and rustics from all round the county and further afield came pouring into Bury on foot and in carriages and gigs. At 11.30 Corder was told to prepare himself. After a walk through the wards of the prison bidding farewell, Corder was taken outside. As he appeared a deathly hush fell over the crowd of thousands and men removed their hats. Corder accepted his fate and the noose was tied about his neck. A rope was cut to release the trap and Corder was sent to his death, the executioner rapidly putting his arms around Corder's middle and pulling him down to speed his end. 'The Red Barn Murder' was arguably the most notorious solved murder case of the nineteenth century, with broadsheets, books, ceramic figurines and even a West End play produced about it.

12 August   **1915**   Woodbridge was bombed by Zeppelin L.10 under the command of Oberleutnant Friedrich Wenke. The Zeppelin dropped four high-explosive and twenty incendiary bombs on the town, killing six and injuring twenty-four.

13 August   **1588**   Edward Rookwood had the honour of entertaining Queen Elizabeth I. During her stay one of her entourage found a statue of the Virgin Mary in the house and brought it to the Queen's notice. The Rookwoods were an ancient Suffolk family, and well known for their Catholic faith. The queen was offended but dealt with the situation by ordering the statue to be burnt 'to the unspeakable joy of everyone'. The hospitality demanded for a visit by the queen would place stress on all but the wealthiest nobles and some never recovered from the debts amassed from a visit by 'Good Queen Bess'. In 1588 Edward Rookwood was imprisoned at Ely for debt and kept there until his death ten years later. With this sort of 'royal treatment' it is hardly surprising that Rookwood's cousin Ambrose became a member of the Gunpowder Plot in 1605.

14 August   **Last Rites**

In August 1878 a 2-year-old boy named Joseph Ramsey died unbaptised at Akenfield. When the bereaved parents contacted George Drury, the local rector, he agreed to have the child buried in the area of the churchyard usually occupied by strangers, still-born infants and suicides and stated that only a simple service of committal would be performed. On the day of the funeral a large cortège from the members of the Baptist community, of which the Ramseys were active members, arrived at the gate of the churchyard. Their minister, Wikham Tozer, was reading the processional scripture when Revd Drury interrupted him and directed the funeral party to proceed immediately to the grave where they could conduct their service. Tozer ignored Drury and carried on the reading. Drury became incensed and insistent and soon an unseemly altercation erupted between the two ministers concluding with Tozer telling Drury to 'Go to hell' and Drury locking the churchyard gates. When Tozer eventually finished the reading, the party found their way through the hedge and finally laid little Joseph to rest. Tozer went on to write a scathing account of the affair in a local newspaper and Drury took him to court claiming £2,000 damages. Drury won the case but was only awarded 40s damages. The legacy of the Akenham burial case had far-reaching implications. It was the pivotal incident that led to the 1880 Burial Law Reform Act which stipulated that all Christians, of whatever denomination, had the right to be buried in a churchyard.

1801 William Baldwin (43), a soldier based at Ipswich, was executed at Ipswich Gaol for highway robbery.   **15 August**

1785 Inscribed on a tablet on the old charnel house in Bury St Edmunds Graveyard: 'Here lies Interred the Body of MARY HASELTON, A Young Maiden of this Town, Born of Roman Catholic Parents and virtuously brought up; Who being in the Act of prayer, Repeating her Vespers, was instantaneously killed by a flash Of lightening August 16th 1785, Aged 9 years.'   **16 August**

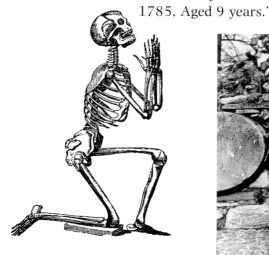

Mary Haselton's memorial on the charnel house in the graveyard at Bury St Edmunds.

17 August **1816** *A day for atonement.* The registers of Fritton recorded Hannah Freeman did penance in the church for defaming the character of Mary Hanham, spinster. On this day in 1822 Robert Bennett (48) of Mellis was executed at Ipswich Gaol for arson. More curiously, exactly nine years to the day in 1833, William Jolly (34) of Eye was also executed at Ipswich Gaol for arson.

18 August **1328** On St Helen's Day, at about midnight, Thomas de Thornham 'with many fugitives and outlaws' came to Bury and took the keys to the gates of the town by force: 'none of the townsmen saying them nay, [they] hurried off to breakfast at Moyse's Hall, and on their way killed Roger Peasenhall, a servant of the Abbey'. When a woman out of Cooks' Street had come to take the price of the breakfast she had sold them she happened to glance into a nearby cellar 'and saw a most horrible devil, as though he were writing'. All of a tremble at his horrible countenance, she drew back the foot which she had put across the threshold, but not without punishment, for instantly that foot was roasted by infernal fire, and fell rotting from her body.

19 August **1851** Ann Mary Cage (41), a widow of Stonham, was executed for murder at Ipswich Gaol.

20 August **1875** An inquest into a fatal accident was held in the Crown and Anchor Hotel at Framlingham. George Warner (19), 'a very steady young man', was in charge of a threshing machine which he was removing for his master, farmer William Webber, from Framlingham to Easton. Coming down Fore Street the incline magnified the pressure of the machine on the horses and they increased their speed. As Webber endeavoured to turn the speeding horses into Farfield Road he was knocked down and 'two wheels of the machine passed up his body over his head, crushing it in a fearful manner and causing instant death'.

21 August **1875** Frederick Page (20) was sent to an asylum after murdering servant girl Fanny Pleasant Clarke at Brantham on the 15 August. After asking to go out for an evening walk she was discovered by a local gardener; she was unconscious and thought to have suffered an horrific beating, and she was 'streaked with blood about the head, arms and hands'. Carried to the kitchen of her master's house she was cleaned up and put to bed. Never regaining full consciousness, she died three days later. During the post-mortem two bullets were found lodged in her brain and another was thought to have passed through the head. The inquest was carried out in the schoolroom. Witness statements soon revealed Fanny had 'kept company' with Frederick Page for some time but showed preference for another brother. When Fanny broke the news to Frederick he literally went insane with jealousy. Brought before magistrates he was ordered to the assizes. Found guilty but insane he was sent to an asylum to be detained at Her Majesty's pleasure.

1914   In the early days of the First World War the British population had to
rapidly become accustomed to some of the wartime restrictions and
rigmaroles imposed to combat threats of invasion or in response to the very
real fear of spies and 'enemies within'. There were numerous near misses
across the country but some incidents ended in tragedy as heard at the
inquest on Herbert Clarke, a GER porter at the Drill Hall, Felixstowe on this
day. In a statement given by Wilson Smith, the doctor who had attended the
deceased, he said Clarke had told him he was returning from the station to
his home at 11 p.m. Passing three sentries he had shown them his pass and
was allowed through. No doubt tired and fed up of such inconveniences,
when challenged a fourth time he answered 'friend' and kept cycling. The
sentry, Edward Kelly, recalled Clarke told him 'not to worry himself', but Kelly
had been given strict orders and shouted his challenge of 'Halt! Friend or foe?'
three times. What exactly happened is unresolved but is probably best
described as a combination of scared and inexperienced soldier and fatigued
railway worker who just wanted to get home after a long day at work. What
is certain is that the sentry rattled off four shots as Clarke tried to make
headway through the gate and, exactly as per his training, when his bullets
had brought down his target the soldier showed him the point of his bayonet.
The sentry retired in tears after giving evidence. The coroner could see the
soldier was acting purely on orders – failure to comply could have met with
court martial and the verdict was directed accordingly. The cause of death on
Clarke was given as 'bayonet and rifle shot wounds delivered by Private Kelly
in the course of his duties'.

Borough of Lowestoft.

TO HOUSEHOLDERS AND THE CIVILIAN POPULATION.

Considering the state of war between Great Britain and
Germany, it becomes my duty to announce the measures taken for the
guidance and safety of the civil population of this Borough, in
case the enemy should attempt an attack on our coast. That there
should be such an attempt is hardly conceivable, but none the less
it would be unwise not to provide as far as human foresight
enables us against every possible contingency. With that view,
arrangements have been made that in addition to the ordinary
police force, at least 150 Special Constables shall be stationed
throughout the Borough, who will advise civilians whether or not
they should remain in their houses or leave the town, and if they
should leave, in what direction and by what means. Arrangements
are being made so that no time would be lost in providing for the
transport of such of the inhabitants as desire to leave to a place
of safety, either by such roads as may be available or by river.

IT IS IMPERATIVE that the instructions of the Police and
Special Constables should be strictly adhered to. Later directions
may be given for observance by civilians who should make themselves
familiar with them beforehand, and it is of the greatest importance
that they should be most carefully and absolutely carried out in
every detail.

I trust that if necessity should arise to put these
directions into operation, they will be carried out with calmness
and courage, and that the civilians of Lowestoft will prove worthy
of their countrymen who have already maintained in the field of
battle the traditions of the British Army.

GOD SAVE THE KING.

J. W. Brooke,
Mayor.

TOWN HALL,
23rd Nov., 1914.

23 AUGUST **1581** John Browne of Halesworth died on this day at the age of 80 years and 25 weeks. His commemorative brass in the church reads 'he had by his only wyffe, with whom he lived 54 years and ffive monethes, six sonnes and ten daughters. He hadd also 65 grandchildren, of who 54 were living at the day of his decease'.

24 AUGUST **1814** *A fateful day over the years!* For some reason some days over the years seem to be more fateful than others. Executed on this day in Suffolk; George Maulkin (59) of Ixworth at Bury for 'unnatural offence'. Joseph Bugg (26) of Martlesham, was executed at Ipswich for arson on this day in 1816. The curse only seems to have been broken by the 'double on the drop' of James Philips (40) and John Wade (35) of Hadleigh who were hanged for burglary before a vast crowd at Bury on this day in 1822.

25 AUGUST **Strange and Horrible Tales of Suffolk**
In the late seventeenth and early years of the nineteenth century it was declared the whole of the Hundred of Stowmarket was remarkable for its appearances of fairy folk. In Hollingworth's *History of Stowmarket*, fairies are recorded as having appeared at a number of houses on Tavern Street and on the old hop-ground near the Bury road. People of repute claimed to have lain wait in hidden places to observe the little people dancing, singing and playing music together. These fairies, it was said, 'were very small people, quite little creatures and very merry. But as soon as they saw anybody they all vanished away. In the houses after they had fled, on going upstairs sparks of fire as bright as stars used to appear under the feet of the persons who disturbed them.'

26 AUGUST **1875** The inquest was held at Claydon on Alice Beatrice Smart, infant child of Charles and Anna Smart. The child's bed was an improvised affair made by placing two chairs together, the front part of the chair being placed near the bed and the back a few inches from a chest. On going upstairs at about 9 p.m. the mother looked in on the babe to find the poor mite had fallen through the back of the chair and was hanging between the ledges of the chair quite dead.

27 AUGUST **1645** *Execution of the Bury 'Witches'.* At the height of his notoriety Matthew Hopkins, 'The Witchfinder General', was in great demand from the larger market towns of eastern England to bring along his team and search for witches. Using all manner of lascivious techniques from intimidation to sleep deprivation, swimming and pricking for 'devil's tits' upon which familiars were suckled, Hopkins found and 'proved' many a 'witch'. Contemporary records state that almost

Matthew Hopkins, Witchfinder General.

200 persons had been detained as suspected witches for the 1645 sessions at Bury St Edmunds. In the 'True relation of the Arraignment of Witches That were Tried, Convicted and Condemned at Sessions at St Edmunds-bury' are listed the following eighteen names as those executed by hanging for witchcraft, at Bury on this day: John Lowes (80-year-old Rector of Brandeston), Thomas and Mary Everard, Mary Bacon, Anne Alderman, Rebecca Morris, Mary Fuller, Mary Clowes, Margery Sparham, Katherine Tooley, Sarah Spinlow, Jane Limstead, Anne Wright, Mary Smith, Jane Rivers, Susan Manners, Mary Skipper and Anne Leech.

The charred remains of the houses on Fore Street, Framlingham, after they burnt to the ground on Saturday 26 August 1905. It was the worst fire in living memory in Framlingham; twenty-seven people were left homeless.

28 AUGUST

1875 *Brisk trade for relic hunters at Brantham.* Following the murder of Fanny Clarke by Frederick Page much media and public attention was given to the case. Newspapers keenly pointed out 'there has been no such murder since that of Maria Marten at Polstead in 1828' (indeed Corder had been executed on 11 August 1828, *see* 11 August entry). The key sites at Polstead had been raided by visitors for souvenirs, the Red Barn being 'almost whittled away'. At Brantham 'there was much to keep the relic hunters busy'. The bloodstained dust on the secluded lane where Fanny was shot was 'carefully gathered up by these pilgrims, little stones have been taken up in match boxes, and leaves of the fences near have also been culled, the preference being given of course to any which may show sign of anything which can be conceived as a spot of blood'.

Strange and Horrible Tales of Suffolk
Suffolk has a considerable history of religious persecution and execution in the name of Church and God. In Christchurch Park, Ipswich, stands a

29 AUGUST

Martyrs' Memorial, Christchurch Park, Ipswich.

monument to the men and women from Ipswich and surrounding villages who were burnt at the stake for their religious beliefs and adherence. Crowds of 2,000 or more would gather on Cornhill to observe the proceedings. Heretics were burnt between the hours of 7 and 10 a.m.; they would be chained to a sixpenny stake by the meat market in front of the Shambles in the south-east corner of Cornhill, an area usually used for another popular public entertainment – bull-baiting. When Nicholas Peke of Earl Stonham was being burnt in 1537, Dr Reading called out 'Peke recant thy opinion and I have thy pardon in my hand' to which Peke replied 'I defy it and thee', sealing his words by spitting out a gobbet of blood from his mouth. Dr Reading was livid and proclaimed to the assembled in the name of the Bishop of Norwich '40 days pardon for sins, to all who would cast a stick into the fire'. Whereupon the assembled gentry drew their swords and set about any tree which would yield a branch and cast them into the fire! (*see also* 8 February and 22 September).

30 AUGUST   1806   Miles Rayner (37) of Ipswich was executed at Ipswich Gaol for horse-stealing.

31 AUGUST   1642   *Pied Pipers of Beccles.* At a time when Beccles was infested with rats, the town port reeve was under pressure to rid the houses of vermin because the plague was feared, but had little to answer the problem. One day a deputation

The tower of Beccles Church, *c.* 1905.

of three, namely Peter Harris the watchmaker, Jonathan Betts a tallow chandler and a pedlar named Samuel Partridge presented an unusual solution to the problem to the port reeve: they would pipe the rats away! The price was steep – 45,000 marks – but they promised they would not claim a penny until the job was successfully carried out. The town elders agreed to the proposal. It transpired later that the men had visited three old hags named Nan Driver, Sally Price and Fanny Barton in their shack by the river and cut a deal to gain the power to charm the rats with pipes. Standing by the river the three men began to pipe, and soon thousands of rats were swarming up the lane to drown themselves in the river. The following day not a rat or even a mouse was to be found in Beccles. Even though the good burgesses of Beccles honoured their side of the deal, none of the three pipers came to claim their money. Perhaps the deal they cut with the hags was more than they bargained for; either way it is said that, ever since, phantom skeletons playing their pipes can still be heard by the river at Beccles on 31 August and so doomed they will play for evermore.

September

The Flodden Field Helmet. This magnificent helmet was worn by Thomas Howard, Earl of Surrey, 2nd Duke of Norfolk when acting as Henry VIII's Lieutenant in the North at the Battle of Flodden Field, 9 September 1513. He stood with a force of about 20,000 against a foe of 30,000 Scots and French. Great bravery was shown on both sides but victory was with Thomas Howard. He retired to his family home of Framlingham Castle where he died in 1524. Howard was laid to rest in Thetford Priory but his helmet remains to this day, high above his son's tomb, in Framlingham Church.

1 SEPTEMBER **1828** By this time a vast trade had built up around the sensation of the Red Barn murder at Polstead (*see* 11 August). Any souvenirs or artefacts associated with the murderer William Corder, his victim Maria Marten or the scene of the crime attracted considerable interest and money. From the minute Corder was taken down from the gallows, considerable sums of money were offered for the rope that hanged him; some accounts state it was sold for a guinea an inch. Corder's dead body was taken to the Shire Hall where in a private room Mr George Creed, the County Surgeon, made an incision and brief examination with a privileged medical audience. Removed to the Nisi Primus Court, Corder's body, wearing only breeches and stockings, was put on public display and later Mr Mizotti of Cambridge and Mr Child of Bungay made casts of the head for phrenological and craniological studies. Returned to Mr Creed, Corder's body was fully dissected. Creed had some of Corder's skin tanned and a book about the case bound therein. This grim artefact along with Corder's scalp with ear still attached, a pair of pistols and other personal items associated with Corder and Maria are still on show at Moyse's Hall Museum. The Red Barn itself and poor Maria's original gravestone were chipped away by grim relic collectors. Corder's skeleton was eventually put on display at the West Suffolk Hospital. It was installed in a glass case, and when approached a mechanism activated the skeleton's arm to point to the hospital funds collection box! As time passed Corder's skull was exchanged for another by a Doctor Kilner who desired the ultimate addition to his extensive Red Barn murder memorabilia collection. Disturbed by a number of increasingly spooky occurrences which left him of the opinion that Corder's ghost had come for his skull, Kilner gave the skull to his friend Dr Hopkins. Minor disasters and eventual financial ruin descended on both doctors. Only when Dr Hopkins struck upon the idea of bribing a gravedigger to give the skull a secret Christian burial in a country churchyard near Bury was the curse lifted and fortunes restored.

Maria Marten's cottage at Polstead, *c.* 1905.

1916 *A fateful day for Bungay.* In 1652 the first Great Fire was to ravage the town and just over 260 years later a German raider airship passed over the town. This time, however, Bungay had a lucky escape. Kapitänleutnant von Buttlar had crossed the Suffolk coast at Lowestoft and followed the path of the River Waveney. Below him he observed a large settlement and dropped several bombs. Nobody was injured and the majority of the bombs fell on Bungay Common near a Royal Engineers encampment. Buttlar's report was somewhat different; in it he claimed to have steered up the Thames estuary, to have been pursued by enemy aircraft and to have encountered a barrage of anti-aircraft fire as he attacked key areas of London!

1658 *Cromwell's head at Woodbridge.* Oliver Cromwell died on this day. After lying in state at Somerset House he was finally buried in Westminister Abbey near his old compatriots, Henry Ireton and John Bradshaw. And so they rested in peace until after the restoration, when Charles II wreaked terrible revenge on the cadavers of those who committed treason against his father. On 30 January 1661 (the twelfth anniversary of his father's execution) the bodies of Cromwell, Ireton and Bradshaw were unceremoniously disinterred, drawn on a sledge to Tyburn, hung until sundown when they were beheaded. Parboiled and covered in pitch, their heads were impaled on spikes at Westminster Hall on the anniversary of Charles I's funeral. There Cromwell's head remained until it was brought down in a gale and was picked up by a sentry. After passing through a number of hands for various amounts of money, including museum proprietor Herr du Puy who informed visitors in 1710 he could command sixty guineas for it, and after being exhibited in a number of curiosity shows, the head was given by the niece of the last show proprietor to the family doctor, Dr Josiah Henry Wilkinson, for safe keeping. She eventually sold it to him and down this family line it was passed to Canon Horace Wilkinson of Woodbridge. During the 1930s, while in the hands of Canon Wilkinson, the head, still on its iron spike and fragment of wooden pole, was scientifically examined by Dr Karl Pearson and Dr G.M. Morant as well Mr A. Dickson-Wright, surgeon, who noted the evidence of the eight axe blows used to remove Cromwell's head, his 'reddish hair' and even 'the historical wart which Cromwell insisted on his portrait painters putting in, and there in the proper place was the depression from which it had been chipped'. The nose had been flattened during the beheading, almost all the teeth were gone and the lips broken to fragments but all the tests and comparisons proved this was the head of Oliver Cromwell. Canon Wilkinson eventually saw to it that Cromwell's head was given a fitting final resting place when he presented it to Cromwell's old seat of learning, Sidney Sussex College at Cambridge. The head resides there to this day in a secret location known only to a few members of staff.

Engraving from a ticket to the London exhibition of the head of the Lord Protector.

4 September

Last Rites

Burial within, or without, the Sanctuary: in most churchyards the preference was to be buried in the south or east; few wanted to be buried in the shady west or especially the north. This parcel of land was often ecclesiastically registered as unconsecrated, the reason being that the superstitious held that the devil would ride from the north on the Day of Judgement and the souls of suicides and undesirables would form some 'occult wall of protection' for the souls of the righteous elsewhere in the churchyard. In many graveyards a row of graves on the extreme verge held the bodies of strangers buried at the parish charge or of others 'considered unfit to associate underground with the good people of the parish'. The Revd Cullum of Hawstead found this practice 'a vulgar superstition' and voiced his contempt of it in his history of the parish and in his will where he insisted he be buried at the north door of his church. Probably the most unusual burial in the county was carried out in the old courtyard of the Bull Hotel at Woodbridge in 1738. George Carlow, the owner of the hotel, was a member of a sect called the Separate Congregation who believed in burial 'within the community'. He left a dole of 20s to buy bread once a year and have it distributed at his grave to the poor. This tradition is still observed to this day.

5 September

1929 George Morley and his girlfriend Nora Plumb were found in their guestroom at the Bull Hotel, Cavendish. The scene was horrific; the whole of Nora's face and the contents of her skull had been blown out by a single shotgun blast. A few feet away lay her lover with the landlord's shotgun between his knees and his skull blasted off from above the eyebrows. PC Talbot, the local bobby who was summoned by the landlord to the scene, requested further assistance from Inspector Hammond at Glemsford. Hammond arrived with PC Kinsey and Dr Ritchie. The details of the scene were recorded and the bodies removed to an outbuilding that was locked for security. At the inquest it was revealed that Nora (25) had been girlfriend to the older George Morley (37) for some time and had been proposed marriage but she could not give a definite answer. Much was made of Morley's outstanding war record: he had been wounded three times, decorated with the Military Medal, mentioned in dispatches and retired as sergeant major. Known as a quiet man, he was well liked and respected in the village of Great Thurlow where he was a gamekeeper. The evidence, however, was clear, and from the measurements and forensic findings, the jury concluded that Morley had wilfully shot Nora, stewed in his thoughts and remorse and then turned the gun on himself.

6 September

1660 The middle of Broad Street in Bury St Edmunds was infested by thousands of spiders of a reddish colour. Spectators judged them to be as many as would fill a peck. Apparently marching together in a strange kind of order they proceeded to Mr Duncomb's house. Many of them got under the door and spun a huge web between the huge door posts. Wrapping themselves in the web they made two great parcels which dangled towards the ground. The servants in the house noticed this and fetching some dry straw laid it under each parcel. When the straw was lit a sudden flame consumed the majority of them. Mr Duncomb, 'a member of the late parliament', believed the spiders were sent to his house by witches.

7 September

1940 The 'Cromwell' codeword (which warned of imminent German invasion) was given in error and scares of German parachutists and landings abounded across the country. From this date rumours began to circulate of large numbers of dead bodies, said to be German troops who had been burned severely by oil barrages, being washed ashore along the south-east coast. One area where the stories of bodies on the beach in 1940 persist to this day is the Shingle Street area of Hollesley Bay. Had a German invasion force been caught in a flame barrage or had it been dealt with swiftly by the Royal Navy? Were the bodies actually those of British servicemen washed up after a training exercise that went horribly wrong? Or was it all black propaganda to warn any potential invader and reassure the British public, in their 'darkest hour', of the anti-invasion defences of Great Britain? There are many questions but many ordinary people with no motive to lie swore they saw numerous unexplained bodies washed up on the beaches in this area of Suffolk in September 1940.

Guarding a washed-up sea mine at Walberswick.

8 September

1905 A report was published of the inquest at Ipswich Asylum on the body of Mark Marshall (75), a retired mariner. It was stated that the deceased had been admitted to the institution the previous Wednesday as a pauper but a search of his boxes revealed various bags found to contain £468 13s in coins.

9 September   **1645**   Mary, known to history as 'Mother' Lakeland, was burnt for witchcraft at Ipswich. According to the published account of her trial and confession she had sold her soul to the Devil, and in return Satan gave her three imps, two little dogs and a mole which she employed in her services. Among the deeds ascribed to this poor soul was the bewitchment of her husband until he died.

She sent one of her dogs to Mr Lawrence and took away his life and the life of one of his children because he owed her 12*s*; she sent a mole to the maid of Mrs Jennings to torment her and take her life because she would not lend her a pin. Her alleged wrath knew no bounds against Mr Beale who was a suitor for one of her grandchildren but had rejected her. She burnt one of his new-built ships and cursed him to take his life; at the time of the trial he was still living, but in misery as literally half his body rotted as he lived. On the day she burnt it was noted

The Ancient House, Ipswich, *c.* 1908. The spirit of Mother Lakeland is said to make herself known here.

that Mr Beale, who had been sent an imp and had a very hard 'bunch of flesh' grown on his thigh in the shape of a dog, had the whole growth simply drop off and recovered remarkably quickly afterwards. Even into modern times a ghost, thought to be that of Mother Lakeland, sporadically gets up to mischief in Ipswich.

9 September   **1822**   *The greatest mail coach robbery of all time?* The London–Ipswich mail coach was carrying a clerk from Alexander & Company whose task was to deliver £30,000 of the bank's own £10, £5 and £1 notes to its Ipswich office. The clerk claimed he watched the box at all times, keeping it beside him while travelling, and on the two refreshment stops left the coach door open so he could observe the box at all times. When the coach arrived at Ipswich the box was found to have been tampered with and when opened proved to have been emptied! Alexander & Company printed a new batch of notes in red and put announcements in the press that none of their notes printed in black should be accepted. The crime remains an unsolved enigma.

10 September   **1515**   Thomas Wolsey, son of an affluent Ipswich butcher, was created a cardinal. A master administrator, Wolsey exercised a marked influence on affairs of state as King Henry VIII followed his counsel and entrusted more power to his hands, until he was given the ultimate state accolade of Lord Chancellor in 1515, a position he held until a year before his death. Wolsey was not liked by the public; he had aroused public hostility with his financial exactions and provoked the enmity of all by the extravagant pomp with which he surrounded himself on public occasions. His origins were used as a term of derision behind his back by many at court, who referred to him as 'son of a butcher'. By 1529 Wolsey was felt by Henry to be 'failing his king'. Wolsey really fell from favour after he failed to

An eighteenth-century engraving of the gateway, all that was left of Thomas Wolsey's College in Ipswich.

obtain the annulment of the king's marriage to Catherine of Aragon. Wolsey died while being escorted by king's commissioners to the Tower of London where he was to answer charges of high treason. His passing was unlamented by all except those in his closest retinue.

1800 On or about this date, after a bad harvest and seven inflationary years of war, a hungry mob ransacked the food stalls and shops around Cornhill, Ipswich. The following week the mob turned its attentions to the tide mill at Stoke Bridge. The Ipswich volunteers were called out to restore order and Batley, the town clerk, read the Riot Act. A pitched battle inside the warehouse saw precious bags of flour thrown about with abandon. The soldiery stood firm and forced the mob out into the churchyard of St Peter's, where fighting turned into a hail of stones and bricks. The crowd were eventually dispersed by mounted troops from St Martin's Barracks.

11 September

1737 Bridgett Applethwaite was laid between the remains of her brother and first husband, Arthur, in Bramfield church. After over four years as a widow she contemplated marriage again but, as her memorial states, 'DEATH forbade the banns'. She was struck 'with an Apoplectick Dart [the same Instrument which had allegedly ended her mother's life]. Touch't the most vital part of her brain she must have fallen Directly to the Ground (as one Thunderstrook) If she had not been Catch't and Supported By her Intended Husband'. There followed a struggle of about sixty hours 'In Terrible Convulsions, Plaintive Groans or Stupefying Sleep Without Recovery of her speech or Sences'. This tragic tale is told in equal detail on her gravestone.

12 September

13 SEPTEMBER **1893** William Whale of London attempted to run, for a wager of £15 to £20, from London to Great Yarmouth via Ipswich. His attempt was to be staged over two days of twelve hours each but sadly he failed by about two hours.

14 SEPTEMBER **1750** *The execution of Black Toby.* The arrival of Sir Robert Rich's Regiment with their fifes, drums and redcoats made quite an impression on the locals of Blythburgh as they marched through the village to make camp. One particularly striking figure was that of Tobias Gill, a tall black drummer. He had a certain dangerous magnetism about him that young ladies loved but parents hated. One night after drinking at Walberswick, he encountered Ann Blakemore. The truth of what happened will never be known but the facts we are left with are that Gill was very drunk and the following morning the strangled body of Ann Blackmore with 'signs of interference' was discovered on Blythburgh Common. Suspicion immediately fell on Gill and while still in a stupor he was arrested and taken to Bury St Edmunds to await trial. Found guilty, he was executed and his body parboiled, tarred and placed in a gibbet cage on the common near the spot where Ann's body had been found. Supposed to be a warning to others, Toby's body drew visitors from far and wide for years to come. This site, although the gibbet is long gone, still has many visitors who come to enjoy a picnic at this popular beauty spot known as 'Toby's Walks'. It is also said that the wheels of a phantom carriage pulled by headless horses whipped up by Toby himself can still be heard on dark, stormy nights.

15 SEPTEMBER **1900** Reports appeared in local newspapers of a triple slaying at Haverhill. Fifteen-year-old Louisa Mizon walked into the upper room of her cottage in Keeble's Yard, off Queen Street, to discover her mother and newborn twins lying on the floor with their throats cut. Nearby on an oak chest lay a bloody razor. Her father, Ellis Backler (he and her mother lived as husband and wife but were not married) was a man who was known as one prone to violent outbursts; he was nowhere to be found. Once the hue and cry was raised Inspector Smith instigated a search and traced Backler to the road near the Plumbers Arms at Denston. The trial at Suffolk Assizes, held at Ipswich, received great public interest and was presented before a courtroom with packed galleries and crowds outside. Much was made of Backler's family history of insanity but it was considered by the Judge that he did know right from wrong and, found guilty, he was sentenced to death – a pronouncement Backler reacted to with 'stolid indifference'. While awaiting his punishment in Ipswich Gaol, news came of his sentence being commuted to confinement in a lunatic asylum 'at Her Majesty's Pleasure'.

1894   One of the great country traditions of the past was to celebrate
marriages in the parish by firing gunpowder on the anvil. Walter Grint, the
Thurlton blacksmith, found his experience of this
tradition was not so lucky. He had poured
gunpowder into the hole on his anvil and
hammered a plug of wood tightly on top.
He then bored a hole in the wood, added a
little more powder and applied a red hot
poker to the powder expecting it to bang
off like a cannon and the plug to disappear
into space. The explosive did not go off.
Leaving the charged anvil for what he
considered a suitable time Grint returned to
examine what had gone wrong. The instant
he bent down his head the charge blew,
'the plug smashing into the eye found
lodgement in its place'. Taken to Beccles
Hospital, when he arrived they did not hold out
much hope for the survival of the other eye either.

16 SEPTEMBER

1835   The report of the commissioners on Ipswich Poorhouses was published
on this day. Meals were shown to consist of bread and cheese every day for
lunch and meat, gravy and suet pudding for supper – hot for three days of
the week, cold for the next three. On Mondays inmates had bread and cheese
for every meal. The cost was estimated as 3*d* per week per pauper. At
St Clements twenty-three residents were recorded in 1835, inmates were
employed in spinning and were paid 5*d* out of every 18*d* earned.

17 SEPTEMBER

The new Ipswich
Workhouse was built
between 1896 and
1899. It cost over
£30,000, could
accommodate 369
inmates and included
an infirmary, receiving
wards and tramp cells.
(Geoffrey Scott)

18 SEPTEMBER

Strange and Horrible Tales of Suffolk

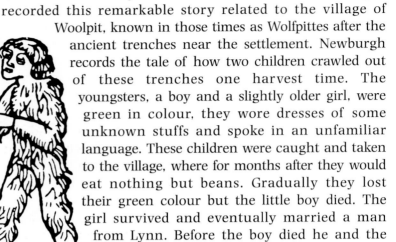

The fifteenth-century chronicler, William of Newburgh, recorded this remarkable story related to the village of Woolpit, known in those times as Wolfpittes after the ancient trenches near the settlement. Newburgh records the tale of how two children crawled out of these trenches one harvest time. The youngsters, a boy and a slightly older girl, were green in colour, they wore dresses of some unknown stuffs and spoke in an unfamiliar language. These children were caught and taken to the village, where for months after they would eat nothing but beans. Gradually they lost their green colour but the little boy died. The girl survived and eventually married a man from Lynn. Before the boy died he and the little girl did learn English and they were able to say they belonged to the land of St Martin in an unknown country. Their country was a Christian land and had churches. There was no sun there, only a faint twilight; but beyond a broad river there lay a land of light. One day they were watching their father's sheep when they heard a loud noise like the ringing of the bells of St Edmunds Monastery. All at once they found themselves in the trenches by the reapers at Woolpit.

19 SEPTEMBER

1892   The inquest into the death of William James Francis, a platelayer on the Great Eastern Railway at Ipswich, was published. The peace of a Saturday afternoon was shattered by Francis's neighbour John James McCabe banging on the back door and shouting, 'Come out you —— thief, you stole the salt.' Francis left by the front door and went to summon the local constable, but returned alone. Soon McCabe appeared again, worse for drink, and the shouting started again. A fight erupted, Mrs Francis came to intervene but she was pushed away by McCabe. She noticed he had something in his hand 'which looked like a pair of curling irons'. She then realised her husband had suffered a blow to the right side of the face and she pulled him inside and locked the door. He died sometime later. At the inquest Drs Vincent and Elliston both gave evidence that death was caused by inflammation of the brain, caused by laceration that could not have been caused by McCabe's fist alone. The jury recorded a verdict of 'wilful murder'.

20 SEPTEMBER

1881   The *Bury and Norwich Post* recorded the inquest into the death of Combs labourer, Walter Green, a man of about 40. Employed to cart wheat on a local farm, the labourers consumed 'an immense quantity of beer during the day'. Witnesses deposed Green had started the day at 6.30 and had consumed at least two pints of his own and one from the foreman by breakfast time. After his breakfast Green brought back a five-pint jugful which he drank between breakfast and dinner. At noon he left for a liquid lunch at the Prince of Wales beerhouse. 'Not quite sober', he consumed another two pints in the afternoon and after work went to Rose Hall where more beer was laid on. Now very drunk he was stumbling around and fell over, striking his head on the barn wall. He was taken home and sat in his chair fast asleep. When he fell from the chair his wife let him sleep it off on the floor. At 10 p.m. he stopped snoring. His wife turned him over; he looked at her but said nothing, and did not appear to be breathing. She summoned a neighbour and called for Mr Harper the surgeon; his assistant, Walker, came in his stead to find all life in Green extinct. The post-mortem found the crack at the base of the skull caused by one of his falls that night and the jury recorded a verdict of 'accidental death'.

1776 As stagecoaches became increasingly equipped to meet the menace of the highwayman with not only armed guards but armed passengers, many gentlemen of the road sought easier prey such as the turnpike toll gates through which the carriages passed. On this night, John Flower, the keeper of the Red Lodge toll gate, was called to open the gates about the hour of 9 o'clock. Used to answering such requests at all hours, Flower left the warmth of his hearth to attend his gates. He was confronted by a masked highwayman who brandished a pistol and demanded the toll money. Before he could answer the request the pistol loosed a shot into the keeper's neck. Stepping over the collapsed body of the gatekeeper, the highwayman entered the tollgate cottage and demanded Mrs Flower hand over the money; once this was in his grasp he fled. Poor old John Flower was not dead, although in great pain and still bleeding. He was trundled along to Mildenhall where a doctor successfully removed the ball.

21 September

The Burning of John Noyes at Laxfield.

1557 John Noyes was executed at Laxfield. Another of 'Bloody Mary's' victims, John Noyes and a few confederates met in secret to worship the Church of England rather than the Church of Rome. Espied in his activities and surprised at his back door he was challenged by Thomas Lovell, Chief Constable of the Hoxne Hundred, Nicholas Stannard and Wolfren Dowsing, 'faithful and catholick Christians'. Arrested by Laxfield parish constables John Jacob and William Stannard, who just happened to be nearby, Noyes was thrown into Eye Dungeon and then carted to Norwich to stand trial for heresy before the Bishop of Norwich. Found guilty he was sentenced to be burnt at the stake. He was transported back to Eye Dungeon and thence to Laxfield, in the middle of the night of the

22 September

21/22 September, to await his fate the following morning. A great crowd assembled to watch the burning of John Noyes. His final words spoke against the idolatry of Catholics: 'They say they can make God of a piece of bread, believe them not!' Foxe's *Martyrs* concludes of the event, 'And so he yielded up his life, and when his body was burned, they made a pit to bury the coals and ashes, and amongst the same they found one of his feet that was unburned, whole up to the ankle, with the hose on, and that they buried with the rest.'

23 September

Suffolk Old Dame's Leechcraft

To 'charm' warts, procure a dodman (snail) and a thorn from a gooseberry bush. Pierce the snail with the thorn and anoint the warts with the shrine from it. Then bury the dodman without removing the thorn from it. As it decays the warts will disappear.

To cure wens or fleshy excrescences pass the hand of a dead body over the part affected on three successive days, the hand of a suicide or executed murderer being deemed more efficacious than that of one who died a natural death. In the days of public executions a hangman could occasionally be bribed to allow a sufferer onto the gallows to enable the wen to be stroked by the hand of the executed felon while he still swung on the rope. This type of action was deeply resented by the crowd who would boo and jeer at the proceedings.

24 September

Bridewells and Gaols visited by Prison Reformer John Howard

Bury St Edmunds Gaol was visited by Howard on five separate occasions between 1774 and 1782. Howard happened to visit when the courtyard was being repaired and made more secure by *chevaux de frise* (defensive obstacles made from a frame with rotating spikes), and noted that no prisoner had use of it without paying a shilling a week. On one side of the courtyard were several rooms for debtors and a workroom. On the other side was a large dungeon down three steps which acted as the day and night room for felons. Howard noted 'men are chained to staples fixed in the barrack-bedsteads'. Another dungeon down a further step or two was seldom used. There was no proper separation of male and female prisoners and there was no straw. According to Howard, 'The late Gaoler told me that in the winter of 1773, five died of the small-pox; no apothecary then but one is appointed since; salary £40.' There was still, however, no infirmary and no bath. A chaplain came to say prayers with prisoners twice a week – his amazing salary was £50. The keeper had no salary and made his money on fees: debtors 8s 8d, felons 6s 8d plus garnish – 'luxuries' like meat, blankets, coal or straw to be bought at inflated prices from the gaoler. The prison even had a licence for beer and wine. Howard sniffed, 'I always found a number of people drinking, as at a common alehouse.' Debtors received no allowances whereas felons were given a threepenny loaf every other day (weight in July 1782, 2lb 6oz). From 5 November to the Saturday before Lady Day, felons had two bushels of coal a week, debtors four; both from a legacy left to the gaol. At the times of the twice-yearly assizes, prisoners of both sexes were brought from Ipswich to the dungeons here to await trial.

RULES,

ORDERS, AND REGULATIONS,

TO BE OBSERVED AND ENFORCED IN

THE GAOL,

AND

HOUSE OF CORRECTION,

FOR THE

LIBERTY OF BURY ST. EDMUND'S,

IN THE COUNTY OF SUFFOLK.

Approved by the Justices in Sessions, July 22, 1805, and
confirmed by the Judges at the subsequent Assizes.

BURY ST. EDMUND'S :
PRINTED BY P. GEDGE, No. 2, HATTER-STREET,
Secretary to the Suffolk and General Country Fire-Office.

RULES, ORDERS, &c.

GAOLER.

1. A Salary shall be paid to the Gaoler, of Three Hundred Pounds a year, for Self and Turnkeys, in lieu of any fee, gratuity, or emolument whatsoever, except such as shall be hereafter specified, or allowed, by the Committee.

2. He shall not, directly or indirectly, be concerned in any other occupation or employment whatsoever, nor have any interest in the contracts for cloathing or feeding the Prisoners.

3. He shall not lodge or board, for hire, in his house, any persons except Prisoners, whose names he shall enter in his Journal.

4. He shall not, either by himself or servants, take, or suffer to be taken, any money or perquisite, for admission to see the Prison or Prisoners, nor on any other account whatever.

5. He shall deliver, at every Quarter Sessions, an account, in regular columns, of all the County Cloathing, specifying what has been

---

Strange and Horrible Tales of Suffolk

25 September

A Dutch prisoner at Woodbridge, in the reign of Charles II, claimed he could discern spirits. On one occasion when the bell tolled for a newly deceased man, this prisoner 'saw' the man and was able to describe the deceased to the parson of the parish who just happened to be with the prisoner at the time. The prisoner told the parson the ghost was between him and the wall; the parson could discern nothing. Approaching the wall purposely the parson was thrown to the floor by invisible hands. Several credible persons put their name to the authenticity of this account.

26 September

1449 Recorded in precise detail on a Canterbury manuscript is an account of a fight between dragons at Little Cornard. The great roars of unknown beasts were heard in the village. A few of the bravest local men, armed with staffs and spears, went to investigate. Arriving at the field from where the noises came they were aghast to see two great dragons, one red and on legs, the other black moving by a serpent-like roll. Twisting around the field, the dragons lunged and clawed at each other, one even breathing fire for over an hour, until both were wounded, but neither emerging as clear victor, they sloped off again: the red dragon to Ballingdon Hill in Essex, south of the Stour; the black one slithering back to Kedlington Hill.

27 September

1876 The reported case of Frederick Gayfer (19) of Ipswich who 'unlawfully wounded' his mother-in-law in a reprisal attack after an argument. At the

Winter Assizes the judge proclaimed Gayfer 'a very dangerous person – a person with vindictive and bad feeling who will go to any length to satisfy your vengeance'. Gayfer was sent down for seven years' penal servitude.

28 September   **1866**   General Tom Thumb and Commodore Nutt visited Ipswich. These two characters were midgets 'discovered' and established by showman Phineas T. Barnum. Born in 1838 as Charles Sherwood Stratton, the son of a Bridgeport carpenter, when taken on by Barnum in 1842 he stood just 25in high and weighed 15lbs. Christened by Barnum as General Tom Thumb, he travelled America and Europe as a living curiosity and was introduced to national leaders such as Abraham Lincoln and Queen Victoria along the way. In 1862 Barnum claims to have paid $30,000 to acquire a new performer – George Washington Morrison 'Commodore' Nutt. Every bit as talented and witty as Tom Thumb, Nutt stood just 29in; they toured as a two-man show. Nutt even acted as best man when Tom Thumb married another midget, Lavinia Warren, in 1863.

'Commodore' Nutt.

29 September   **1557**   An unfortunate fellow named John Jarvis was heard to say 'Good Lord, how the sinews of his arms shrink up!' at the burning of John Noyes at Laxfield (*see* 22 September). At any other time his exclamation would have caught just the disapproving eye of any pious person or cleric but unfortunately Jarvis spoke out of turn at a place where there were many hardline religious zealots present and he was in court before his feet could touch the ground. At the first hearing he denied saying the words and his father and master were bound for £5 each that he should be forthcoming at all times. On this day Jarvis appeared before Justices Thurston and Keane at their sitting in the Hoxne Hundred. They judged him guilty and sentenced him to be set in the stocks the next Saturday, market-day, and then stripped and whipped about the market place. Jarvis's master craved the indulgence of the constables and persuaded them to show mercy. John Jarvis was thus sat in the stocks on the Sunday and whipped about the marketplace with a three-tailed dog-whip instead.

30 September   **1825**   The diary entry for Charles Freeman of Stowupland Hall for this day states: 'My wife was put to be at noon of a stillborn male child.' Nothing more is said, not even a mention of a burial service, but then many churches would not allow burial of such babies because they were unbaptised. When the hall was sold after the Second World War, renovations and alterations were carried out which included the removal of some of the old plaster in the entrance hall, which when tapped sounded hollow. Behind was revealed a small alcove in which the tiny body of a baby had been walled up many years before.

OCTOBER

No village would have been complete without its whipping post and stocks,
like these at Ufford, *c.* 1910.

1 OCTOBER **1887** The Revd William Meymott Farley (73), Rector of Cretingham, was murdered in his bed by his Curate, Revd A.E. Gilbert-Cooper, who wielded a cut-throat razor on his elderly victim. At the subsequent inquest he looked totally bewildered and would not accept that Revd Farley was dead. At the trial it soon became evident the curate had frequent bouts of eccentric behaviour, said to be as a result of the severe sunstroke he had suffered as a boy in India. Found guilty but of unsound mind he was sent to Broadmoor Prison Asylum for the rest of his life.

2 OCTOBER **1888** *A pub brawl.* During a quiet night in the Woolpack Inn at Haverhill, the landlord, Fuller Chamberlain, was in the taproom with Frank Farrant when local labourer, Arthur Hall (20), called for beer. When presented with his pint, Hall stated he only had three-halfpence in his pocket to pay. Chamberlain took the beer back and reminded him he had been refused credit for bad debts in the pub before. Hall stated he wanted a quiet word with Chamberlain; the landlord told him to speak on. Hall asked if the landlord remembered him hitting him, to which Chamberlain said, 'I don't want any of your nonsense to-night.' Hall levelled up close to Chamberlain, stating, 'You ——, I'll rip your —— —— up!' Putting down his pint pots, Chamberlain saw Hall had a knife in his hand. He hit Hall but the ruffian got up again and before he knew it the blade was cutting across Chamberlain's neck. In the ensuing struggle Hall's fingers ended up in Chamberlain's mouth, 'trying to rend it'. Chamberlain bit with all his might and floored Hall until the constable arrived to take him into custody. The report of this fracas concludes: 'Farrant stood smoking his pipe throughout'. The jury at the Assizes found Hall guilty of wounding with intent to do bodily harm. Sentence – 12 months penal servitude with hard labour.

3 OCTOBER **1804** The inquest was held into the death of a young child named Mary Mills at Friston. Mary was playing with other children when an escaped fighting cock was seen to fly up at the child and peck her with its beak and scratch with its feet much in the way it would attack another cock in the pit. The girl was knocked to the ground and it was some time before an adult could reach the child and fend off the bird. The child was seen to have blood streaming from her eyes, nose, mouth and head. Taken home the poor little mite did not survive and the coroner had to return a verdict of accidental death – 'killed by a fighting cock'.

4 OCTOBER **1905** *The Somerleyton outrage.* At about the hour of seven in the morning a fisherman named James 'Jumbo' Ecclestone who was living at Somerleyton attempted to take his life by diving into the River Waveney. He was saved from the rushing waters by marshman James Jackson and removed to the shore where he was resuscitated. As this dramatic action took place Mr Ward, the landlord of the Duke's Head, raised the alarm that his barmaid, Emma Chipperfield, had been seriously attacked. Dr Bell was summoned and took two hours to dress the eleven wounds about her face, neck and body which had been inflicted by Ecclestone with his clasp knife. Despite the hail of wounds, by some miracle no stab proved fatal, despite her lung being punctured and one cut to a finger requiring amputation. Distracted in his attack by the arrival of Maud Heap, who heard the screams, Ecclestone had run from the scene to throw himself in the river. The news of his hideous deed reached the riverbank shortly after Ecclestone's revival and he was soon in custody. In a case heard at the winter assizes the judge said he would wait to see if Emma recovered from her wounds and pass sentence accordingly. Thankfully Emma did recover, but by this recovery Ecclestone avoided the gallows and was sentenced to twenty years' penal servitude.

1871 Thirteen-year-old Alfred Amos was caught stealing apples from an orchard by Head Constable Sach of Sudbury Borough Police and was sentenced to one months' hard labour. **5 OCTOBER**

1811 Reports were circulated of the death of Thomas Colson, an eccentric character of Ipswich, more generally known as Robinson Crusoe. Once a member of the Suffolk Militia and a stocking weaver, he became a fisherman on the Orwell. His boat was a mass of patches and to eke out his meagre living, he fished in all weathers. 'Subject to violent chronic complaints, and his mind somewhat distempered, his figure tall and thin, with meagre countenance and piercing blue eyes' he was aptly described: **6 OCTOBER**

> With squalid garments round him flung,
> And o'er his bending shoulders hung
> A string of perforated stones
> With knots of elm and horses bones.
> He dreams that wizards, leagued with hell,
> Have o'er him cast their deadly spell,
> Though pinching pains his limbs endure,
> He holds his life by charms secure,
> And while he feels the torturing ban,
> No wave can drown the spell-bound man.

Tragically, his boat was driven onto 'the Ooze' by a storm on 3 October. Totally convinced of the efficacy in the charms with which he surrounded himself, he obstinately refused to leave his vessel, so when the ebb tide came he and his little boat were swept into deep water and poor Robinson sank to rise no more.

1767 *Judgement of murder by employers.* Mary Larter was brought to Framlingham Workhouse 'in a bad way'; she sat for about three hours until she asked her friend Mary Fiske to lead her to bed where she died sometime later. The stories Mary Larter told of the events leading up to her death left her friends in no doubt of the cause of her demise. Days before, while churning butter at her Master Sherman's, she told her mistress she felt so ill she could not carry on, upon which her mistress insisted she carry on even if 'she dropped down dead'. After finishing the churning Mary collapsed in a faint. **7 OCTOBER**

The poorhouse inside the ruinous castle walls at Framlingham, c. 1770.

The following day her master hit her with her mistress's riding whip because he thought she could milk faster. The following day her mistress pushed her against the pump, causing her nose and mouth to bleed; unable to get up when ordered, her mistress got her riding whip again, dragged her till she got up and whipped her again. Carried to the magistrate her treatment was brought to the notice of the law. When the inquest into her death was called the jury was left in no doubt and delivered the verdict of 'murder by employers'.

8 OCTOBER

1797 *He literally drank himself to death*. William Brook was a man 'low in spirits'. He had taken to drinking, and those who knew him were concerned about what he was doing to himself. On the morning of 7 October he had gone to his local inn at Hasketon and bought a bottle and a quart of brandy. By lunchtime Brook's wife was concerned and a search was called. Brook's daughter and one of her little friends discovered Brook 'lying grublings' (face down) in the stackyard. His legs were crossed and his face buried in the mud. Seeing his 'face was very black', farmhand Daniel Richmond was called and he turned Brook over to find him 'quite dead'. The inquest was held the next day and the verdict passed was clear – natural death by excessive drinking.

1870 Walter Chambers (24) accidentally shot his sweetheart, Eliza Spurgin (22), at his home by Fraser's Machine Rooms, St Margaret's, Ipswich. Chambers, who was a good shot and serving member of the 1st Suffolk Rifle Volunteer Corps, had been competing at the racecourse in the monthly shooting challenge cup. All were sure he had cleared his rifle before leaving the butts. He returned home and placed the rifle on the copper in the sitting room. He called on his sweetheart, Eliza, they 'walked out' for the evening and she returned the next day to prepare and share Sunday lunch with the Chambers. The family gathered around the table and, having enjoyed the main course, the apple turnovers on their way, Walter Chambers spied the rifle and reached across his father to pick it up and put it away. With the rifle hardly under his arm it discharged its round at close range to Eliza who, 'horribly mutilated, sank from her chair'. Mr Hammond, the surgeon, was called but there was nothing to be done. He stated at the inquest that 'by the side of the fearfully mutilated head was a mass of brains, which had fallen out of the skull, from which the forehead and left side had been carried by the bullet. The brains were also scattered in all directions about the room.'

Suffolk Old Dame's Leechcraft

To cure nightmares and ward off the evil eye, hang a flintstone with a natural hole in it over the head of your bed. Another remedy is, before you go to bed, place your shoes carefully by the bedside 'coming and going', that is, with the heel of one pointing in the direction of the toe of the other, and then you will be sure to sleep quietly and well.

Strange and Horrible Tales of Suffolk

Great Bradley was home to generations of the Nice family, who were the local corn millers. Hanslip Nice had built the first of their family mills in 1839. This mill served the scattered and quite isolated community very well until 1908 when it really needed considerable renovation. Jo Nice, a descendant of Hanslip, owned the mill at the time and put every penny he had into the restoration. Renovations were going well and were almost complete when a great storm raged over the village and lightning struck the sails, causing extensive damage to the mill. The mill was not insured, and Jo had spent every penny he had on it. Out of his wits with desperation a few days later, poor Jo Nice hanged himself.

1870 *The last joust in Suffolk?* A report of an extraordinary case of fighting between two farmers on horseback was brought before magistrates at Bury St Edmunds. George Palmer, farmer of Hawstead, was charged with assaulting neighbouring farmer William Orbell. Orbell claimed some of Palmer's bullocks had strayed onto his fields. Hailing Palmer by his nickname, Orbell was ignored. Saddling his horse, Orbell went to discuss the matter with his friend and confidante Mr Barrett of Hardwick. The aggrieved farmers passed each other, Orbell on the road and Palmer in his field; 'They then blackguarded each other.' Palmer threatened to hit Orbell; Orbell dared him. Palmer 'went at the complainant like a bullock' and they set about each other with fists and sticks, both remaining on horseback. Tiring, they came to a hiatus and gathered their breath. Palmer shouted, 'Let's have another round or two'; that said 'into one another again they went like smoke, like tinder, like soldiers'. Orbell claimed Palmer called to his men in the field to help; Orbell took this chance to pick up his hat and make his escape. Taking out a summons on Palmer, Orbell appeared in court 'with his face covered in plaster and the remains of a black eye'. Palmer's wounds were also vouched for by Mr Image. After a long deliberation Palmer was fined 6*d*; both parties had to pay their own costs and were bound over to keep the peace for six months.

13 OCTOBER **Bridewells and Gaols visited by Prison Reformer John Howard**
Bury Bridewell (now Moyse's Hall Museum) was visited on five occasions between 1774 and 1782, with just one or two prisoners within on each visit. Howard says of the building, 'it is said, in former times [to have been] a Jewish Synagogue'. A large workroom was recorded along with a room for men and another, separate room for women; 'all upstairs and out of repair'. A small court was noted measuring 13ft by 9ft with no water supply. The keeper's salary was £6; each prisoner paid fourpence for straw and there were fees of 1*s*.

14 OCTOBER **1871** Usually commencing about the second week in October and with roots going back over almost 600 years, the Bury Autumn Fair was finally abolished following increasing complaints about its bawdy and raucous nature. The fair had been colloquially known as the marriage market for years. Daniel Defoe made insinuations about the virtue of the ladies who attended. In 1802 fourteen constables received 5*s* each for keeping order at the fair. By the early nineteenth century the fair took a month to set up, lasted for about four weeks and took a week to take down and clear up and local traders really had had enough. John Glyde junior commented of the fair, 'its great attractions being petty shows, roundabouts, gingerbread stalls and toys. It is a perfect nuisance to the respectable inhabitants of the town.'

15 OCTOBER **1825** Madame Tussaud brought her travelling exhibition to Bury Fair; she had previously brought it in 1818, and on both occasions proved to be one of the star attractions. Particular interest was shown in her 'Separate Room' which was offered for a further 6*d*. In it were the casts of the heads she and her mentor Dr Phillipe Curtius took from the guillotined aristocrats during the French Revolution. With these casts were life-size representations of notorious criminals of the day, instruments of torture, and relics associated with some of the criminals and their crimes. Eventually when Madame Tussaud travelled no more she based herself on the corner of Baker Street and Portman Square and the separate room became the Chamber of Horrors at Madame Tussauds Waxwork Museum, where the cold glass eyes of killers may still be stared into today!

1769   An advertisement for Bury Fair stated: 'To the Nobility, Gentry etc, who are admirers of the extraordinary productions of nature. To be Seen during Bury Fair, at the bottom of Angel Hill, Maria Tereza, the amazing Corsican Fairy, who has the honour of being shown three times before their Majesties. She is only 34 inches high, weighs but 26lbs, and is allowed to be the finest display of Human Nature in Minature that was ever shown in England. To be seen from ten in the morning till nine at night. Gentlemen and Ladies, one shilling; servants etc., sixpence.'

16 OCTOBER

1173   *The Battle of Bury St Edmunds.* In reality this conflict occurred at the nearby village of Fornham All Saints. Robert Whitehands, Earl of Leicester, had raised an army of 3,000 Flemings against Henry II in sympathy for his royal sons. After landing at Walton, near Ipswich, Whitehands and his troops marched to Framlingham Castle where they were welcomed by Hugh Bigod. Mustering more troops and fortified by the sacking of Haughley Castle they marched on Bury, met at Fornham by the king's forces led by Humphrey de Boun. These soldiers had been blooded in their victories against the Scots, surprised Whitehands at Fornham, and forced him back to Fornham St Genevive. Whitehands' entire force was either killed or taken prisoner after a brave final stand in the church. The bones of about forty of the soldiers laid head-to-head were discovered in a mound near the church in the eighteenth century.

17 OCTOBER

Framlingham Castle, *c.* 1790.

18 OCTOBER   **1859**   Bill posters appeared in towns and villages along the River Orwell advertising a feat to be enacted on this day. A man was to walk on the river from Stoke Bridge to the Griffin and there would offer several pairs of his miraculous boots for sale. Thousands came from far and wide and lined the banks of the river in anticipation of observing this momentous event. All were left simply hanging around; hours passed by before most realised this was a hoax.

19 OCTOBER   **1894**   *Caught in the act!* A labourer at Coppin's Farm, Washbrook, beginning his day's work, noticed a loose-box in the stable. Upon entering it he found a man prostrate on the ground, weltering in blood which had clotted upon his features. Removed to a barn, a doctor was called, but he arrived only in time to pronounce him dead. Enquiries named the man as John Cole, a labourer formerly in Coppin's employ. Cole knew that several fowls roosted on the railings of the loose-box and, curiously, since he had left, their numbers had dwindled to one. Reaching up for this last bird, he had undoubtedly brought about his demise. Grasped in his hands were the wing feathers of the bird, while beside the body when it was found was the bird with dislocated leg and other injuries. It was surmised that when Cole grabbed her she fluttered and startled a colt, which kicked the man with such force it smashed both his jaw and skull. At the inquest a verdict of accidental death was returned.

20 OCTOBER   **1871**   The report was published of the inquest held under F.B. Marriott, Coroner, at King's Head Inn, Laxfield, into a fatal threshing-machine accident. Jonathan Read, a 25-year-old labourer, was engaged on Mr Foster's Farm threshing barley. Standing on the top of the machine, his foot slipped and he fell into the drum. He was extracted as quickly as possible and conveyed home but he was losing copious amounts of blood all the way. Dr Crickman was called and he concluded the best course of action was to amputate Read's mangled leg but 'the poor fellow lingered but a short time afterwards'. The jury returned a verdict of accidental death with a recommendation to threshing-machine manufacturers to devise some plan to prevent these recurring accidents. As an aside, local folklore states the blood from this fellow stained areas of the path taken to his home and they were apparent for many years afterwards.

21 OCTOBER   **1770**   Herman Boaz appeared at Bury St Edmunds Theatre. His act consisted first of producing a live pigeon, which he suspended by a garter from the ceiling, the shadow of the pigeon being reflected against the wall by a candle. Boaz then took a sword and by drawing it across the neck of the shadow cut off the real head of the pigeon which was at least six yards away. Other delights included Boaz eating fragments of glass and a pound of tenpenny nails; Boaz encouraged a member of the audience to strike his calf until blood appeared, when the wound would be observed to heal 'in less than three minutes'. Then, after performing card tricks, he proceeded to eat the entire deck, swilled down with a glass of wine, followed by him munching through the glass and decanter 'by way of digestion'. His advert concluded with a note, 'Mr. Boaz will continue to exhibit in Bury every evening during next week, at seven o'clock; but as Methodists and People of Weak Minds in town have imagined he deals with a demon, or something supernatural, he here solemnly declares to such that their notion is utterly false.'

17, ST. NICHOLAS STREET, IPSWICH.

J. BOYCE, SANITARY PLUMBER,

Superintends all Sanitary Work, and having studied the business on scientific principles, is prepared to give reasons for any improvements he may suggest.

Water Closets are the most neglected part of the house, and should be the most cared for ; to prevent Typhoid, Diptheria, and other Fevers, have your Plumber clean your W.C. once a year —the best time is the Autumn.

Orders Respectfully Solicited.

This advertisement from 1885 advises householders to let the plumber clean your toilet – once a year!

22 OCTOBER 1678 An epitaph in Theberton churchyard reads:

> Here is a stone to sit upon,
> Underwich lies in hope to rise on ye day of blisse and happiness
> Honest John, the son of William Fenn Clarke,
> And late Rector of this Parish.
> Being turned out of his living
> And sequestred for his loyalty to his late King Charles the First,
> He departed this life 22 of October. Anno Dom., 1678

23 OCTOBER 1875 Reports began to be published of the death of 'Shelly' Cook, a 3ft dwarf and well-known Lowestoft character. Poor Shelly had often been put in the cells of the local police station to sleep off his state of intoxication. This happened not so much because of his personal spending on drink but because of his short stature; for the sport and amusement of local 'wags' he would be bought drinks until helplessly drunk. His plight was noticed by well-meaning local 'blue ribboners' – teetotal chapelfolk who guided him away from those who would lead him astray. While going to chapel, Bible tucked under his arm, one evening, 'he fell upon tempters' and was bought many a drink by his 'old friends' at the local hostelries. Shelly was totally 'bladdered' by the time he was transported back to his sisters' house in a wheelbarrow and unceremoniously tipped out on the kitchen floor to sleep it off. Tragically Shelly did not wake up in the morning. Sixty-five-year-old Shelly had passed away. Given a very fine and well-attended funeral, no doubt he would have enjoyed the thought of his inquest having been held at the Fox and Hounds Inn.

24 OCTOBER 1887 *A case of bigamy!* Country labourer Thomas Wolsey married Esther Jane Causton at Palgrave on this day. All seemed well until Esther pressed Thomas about his previous wife; he assured her had not seen or heard from her in over ten years. The wife question was still in the back of her mind when, about nine weeks into their marriage, Thomas let slip that he had actually seen his first wife alive and well in Yorkshire while staying there shortly before he and Esther were married. Esther stormed out and soon found a man in Thrandeston who married a sister of Wolsey's first wife and who remembered Wolsey marrying at Thrandeston in 1857! At the assizes in July 1888 the case for bigamy was proved and Wolsey received a firm rebuke from the judge who sentenced him to imprisonment for one month.

25 OCTOBER 1915 H.W. Miller, a well-known Ipswich solicitor, was sentenced to three years' penal servitude for extensive frauds.

26 OCTOBER 1909 The village of Reydon hit national headlines after a massive gale blew a French couple in a hot air balloon the 800 miles from Nancy in Lorraine, across the North Sea, eventually to land near Reydon Grove.

The male passenger left the basket of the balloon unharmed but the lady, who had baled out at Potter's Bridge, was slightly injured.

Strange and Horrible Tales of Suffolk

27 OCTOBER

Margaret Matthews was the daughter of a Lavenham swordmaker. The trade of her father's calling being totally unsuitable for a lady, she teamed up with Thomas Rumbold and together they terrorised the roads of Suffolk and Essex as highwaymen. Retiring on her illicit earnings, Margaret spent her last years in Norwich, where she eventually died from dropsy in 1688. Rumbold kept up his life of robbery, deceptions and cheating until the law eventually caught up with him and he swung at Tyburn in 1689.

Below: Stand and deliver!

1893 From *History of Sudbury*: 'About half past seven . . . what was considered at the time to be a wild and uncharitable rumour spread through the town that a well-known inhabitant had absconded. Since the death of his father, Henry Cronin Pratt had been actuary of the Sudbury Savings Bank. On the Monday he sent his Clerk to Colchester with a bag, telling him that he would drive out and meet him at Colchester Station about 5 p.m. There he

28 OCTOBER

took possession of the bag which Barwick, the clerk, had noticed was very heavy, and shook him by the hand saying, "Good-bye Joe! Take care of yourself." Pratt booked a passage on SS *Cambridge* and, on arrival at the Hook of Holland, his personal bag, watch and chain and card-case with some papers were found in his cabin, but the owner had disappeared. Moore, the steward, said it had been quite possible for Pratt to have gone ashore, quite unobserved, at Rotterdam. When the accounts of the Bank were audited the deficiency was found to be £17,000, approximately half the capital.' The trustees made large contributions and were able to pay out 17*s* 6*d* in the pound to the depositors. Pratt was never found.

29 OCTOBER **1882** Clearing up, repairs and salvage continued apace at Lowestoft after the day which became known as 'Black Saturday'. This was no ordinary storm; in a tempest of lashing rain and wind 'akin to the Cape', the fishing-boats, schooners and brigs in the harbour were whipped up and smashed together in the maelstrom. Some were grounded while others foundered in the water. Casualties included the *Warrior Queen* from Newcastle, which went down with all hands, and the brig *Sovereign* from which seven crew were lost on the infamous Newcome Sands. By 29 October sixty

Shattered ships in Lowestoft harbour after the storm, 29 October 1882.

rescued seamen were thankful for their lives as they took up refuge at the Lowestoft sailors' home. First reports stated that within three miles of Lowestoft harbour at least sixteen vessels were wrecked and thirty lives had been lost.

1757 The death of Admiral Edward Vernon of Orwell Park. The hero of the Battle of Porto Bello in 1739, he was known to the sailors in the British Navy as 'Old Grog' on account of the old grogram cloak he unfailingly wore on the quarterdeck. His name also became attached to his policy of mixing water with the brandy or rum ration in his fleet. An unpopular policy in its day, the name stuck, and even today glasses of 'Grog' are raised with a wry smile by sailors past and present. Vernon is buried with a surprising number of other naval and military leaders in the charming church of Nacton.

30 OCTOBER

All Hallows Eve

On this night above all others, scary and spooky tales passed down the generations are recounted by the fireside. One such tale told in the late nineteenth and early twentieth centuries would be of the 'pinning' of a local suicide. Until the 1850s people who committed suicide could not be buried in consecrated ground but rather in a separate, distant area in the north of the churchyard, where the body would be laid face down, facing west. Many believed the restless spirits of those who took their own lives would 'walk' to harass those they left behind; thus suicides would be buried away from the town or village at a four-way crossroads so the ghost would not know which path to take to return. To ensure the body and ghost stayed down it would be 'pinned' with an oaken stake through the heart (a practice prohibited by Act of Parliament in 1823). Crowds would gather around the local sexton as he performed this duty at the wayside grave; even children would risk the wrath of their parents by creeping along and looking through the legs of those assembled at the grim rite. There are a number of well-attested instances of this being carried out in Suffolk. The *Ipswich Journal* of 4 October 1783 records the case of Ballingdon millwright Mr Hurwood, who committed 'self-murder' by taking arsenic in a fit of discontent. He was 'buried at the cross-way, with a stake driven through his body, near the Pound on Ballingdon Hill'. In 1794 Thomas Adams, an inmate of the Shipmeadow workhouse, stabbed himself with a penknife in the body and neck. He died immediately and the inquest adjudged 'wilful murder': Adams was buried beside the highway with a stake driven through his heart.

31 OCTOBER

Do not be tempted to doubt these tales. One of the most famous wayside graves is at an old pathway crossroads near Kesgrave. John Dobbs had hanged himself in a fit of despair in a nearby barn on the Kesgrave Hall estate. After he had been buried and pinned by the wayside his grave mound became the subject of many local tales. Over the years the tales got taller and more fanciful to the extent that some of the younger bucks did not believe there was anyone buried under there at all. One night after a Harvest Horkey at the

Dobbs' grave.

Bell a few hardy boys, fortified with fine Suffolk ales, went to investigate. They dug down into the mound and soon found the bones of poor John Dobbs. Most took flight and ran off but one particularly hard lad reached into Dobbs' jaw, took a tooth as a souvenir and wore it on his watch-chain for years after.

NOVEMBER

The unveiling of the gravestone of murdered PC Ebenezer Tye in
Halesworth graveyard, 1862. *(Suffolk Constabulary Archives)*

1 NOVEMBER **1894** *The Suffolk Slasher*. Reports of the Suffolk Autumn Assizes included the Lowestoft stabbing case. George Ruthven (22), a fisherman, was indicted for feloniously wounding Sarah Stangroom, Elizabeth Allerton and Samuel Hawes on 16 June. The story emerged that Mr and Mrs Stangroom were walking down London Road, Lowestoft, when the prisoner came running towards them and before they knew what happened he struck Mrs Stangroom in the breast with a concealed blade. Mr Stangroom challenged Ruthven but he ran off, pursued by Mr Stangroom. After 200 yards Ruthven turned and asked Stangroom what the — he wanted and struck him across the nose with his arm. With similar slash attacks already perpetrated on Allerton and Hawes the same evening the police were on the lookout and soon arrived at the altercation when Ruthven was manhandled into custody. At the assizes Ruthven was found guilty of the attacks but was given the surprisingly lenient sentence of six weeks with hard labour.

2 NOVEMBER **1914** William Smith (52), popular schoolmaster at Wangford School, took his own life by cutting his throat. His premature end was brought about through the spy fears and rabid anti-German feelings which permeated Britain in the closing months of 1914 after war had broken out on 4 August. Shortly before the outbreak of war, Smith's son had been studying languages in Aachen, and by exchange visit two young girls had come over to Wangford to learn English. On the outbreak of war the whole situation was twisted by malicious and thoughtless village gossip. The girls were spies, Smith was an agent himself, and his whole family would have to go into detention under the Defence of the Realm Act! Smith's involvement with Germany, however innocent, meant he would be liable to action under the Defence of the Realm Act, and Chief Constable Mayne of the East Suffolk Police thought it best all round if Smith and his family just be ordered to move to another part of the country. For Smith, his thirty years in the village and building up a good school was his life. No doubt feeling his reputation had also been systematically destroyed, he took his own life. His death and the following inquest pricked the consciences of the local people, who turned out *en masse* for his funeral.

3 NOVEMBER **1807** Louis XVIII, King of France, arrived at the Great White Horse, Ipswich, on his way from Yarmouth to Essex. Living in exile in Westphalia when Louis XVI was guillotined in 1793, he declared himself Regent for his nephew, the boy king Louis XVII. When the 10-year-old king died in prison on 8 June 1795, Louis Stanislas Xavier proclaimed himself King Louis XVIII and bided his time around Europe until he gained the French throne in 1814. Undoubtedly the most hideously obese of all the Bourbons, he made desperate attempts to deflect attention from his size by over-dressing in extravagant clothes. When the Prince Regent invested the new French King with the Order of the Garter, he discovered Louis had an elephantine knee. The prince referred to the experience as like 'fastening a sash around a young man's waist'. Having fled Paris for 100 days after the return of Napoleon, Louis took up his throne permanently after Napoleon's final defeat at Waterloo and remained king until his death on 16 September 1824. One cannot help but wonder if the Great White Horse had such ample facilities that it attracted Daniel Lambert when he exhibited himself in Ipswich in 1809. Visiting the town in his reinforced coach, Lambert weighed 52st and measured 9ft 4in around the waist, each leg a phenomenal 3ft 1in at the thigh.

1888 Stradishall labourer George Chapman (30) had an argument with his girlfriend, Mary Ann Dearsley. In the midst of his rage he threw 'certain corrosive fluid at her with intent to burn her or do grievous bodily harm'. Pleading guilty to this horrible act at the Suffolk Winter Assizes at County Hall, Ipswich, Chapman was given two months' penal servitude.

4 NOVEMBER

1909 *Records as long as your arm.* A report of the Ixworth Petty Sessions describes how George, John and Herbert Whistlecraft of Rickinghall Inferior stood on separate accounts of breaches of the game laws. John Whistlecraft (26) was summoned for trespass in search of game on farmer Brother's land at Wattisfield on 22 October. Shots had been heard and pheasants were known to have been in the area. John was fined *2s 6d* with *7s 6d* costs. Herbert Whistlecraft (28) was summoned for unlawfully killing a pheasant on the grounds of Redgrave Hall on 11 October. With eighteen previous convictions recorded, he was fined £1 with *10s 4d* costs. Declining to pay he was committed to prison. George 'Joe' Whistlecraft (31) was summoned for trespass in search of game at Cork Wood, Rickinghall Inferior on 19 October. Seeing Arthur Wallace, the rat-catcher, who had reported him on 19 October at the same place on 21 October, George threatened to kill Arthur, followed the threat with a hail of punches and again threatened to kill Wallace 'whom he struck with a spud'. Superintendent Peck said forty-two previous convictions had been recorded against George Whistlecraft. He was fined a total of £1 *12s 6d* and *7s 9d* costs and one month's hard labour (*see* 8 December).

5 NOVEMBER

1906 *The Heveningham pond mystery.* In the early hours of this day the body of a little girl believed to be about 5 years of age was found in a water-filled pit at Heveningham, near Halesworth. The child had been strangled, a piece of lace was found to be still wound around her neck, and she was distinctive because she had a cataract on her right eye and suffered the bow-legs of rickets. At the inquest held at White House Farm the child was identified as one Annie Palmer. She was remembered by officials at Bulcamp Workhouse as a little girl who had come into the casuals ward with her grandparents on 11 October. Rapid investigations were made and the elderly couple were traced to Norwich, where Annie Palmer was also found alive and well – and with no sign of the ailments suffered by the dead child! Suffolk Police then embarked on meticulous local enquiries. A woman named Louisa Pierce who had an illegitimate child and family still in the area was traced to an address in Kingston-upon-Thames where she had moved in May 1904. Her child, named Ethel Maude was 7 years old and had suffered from rickets and had a 'blind' right eye. Since the mother had found her fancy man in Kingston, the

6 NOVEMBER

Dragging the pond at Heveningham, 1906.

poor, sickly little girl had been passed from pillar to post among relatives, and eventually Louisa said she would take the child to a children's home in Eastbourne. Enquiries soon revealed witnesses who identified Louisa as being in the area of Heveningham on the evening of 5 November carrying a child. Further evidence of fragments of clothes matching those of the murdered child were found in Louisa's effects, and there was no sign of her child at Eastbourne. Despite insisting her child would be found, the evidence was clearly stacked against Louisa and at her trial the following January she was found guilty of the murder of her child and sentenced to death, later commuted to imprisonment 'at His Majesty's Pleasure'.

7 NOVEMBER   1876   Philander Smith, under-gamekeeper to Mr Crawford of Knettishall Hall, was watching game with Oliver Houghton in a plantation called the Larches. About a hundred yards away the report of a shotgun was heard. Running to the scene, Smith saw three men and had a good look in the moonlight at one of them – Ben Annas. Stones were hailed on the keepers, Houghton was struck in the middle of the head and briefly knocked insensible, and the poachers made their escape. Report was made to PC George Barnes who investigated the case and found witnesses who put Annas at the scene with other men, one of whom was seen to have a gun but only Annas's name was forthcoming. Annas did not sell out his fellow poachers and faced the magistrates alone. The bench concluded: 'These kind of exploits will not answer any good purpose for you may depend upon it they will get you into trouble. You will be sentenced to six months' imprisonment.'

1894 The report of the inquest on the wife of Tampion Cunnell of Athelington, near Eye. The deceased, who left a husband and two children, had been suffering from influenza. First to come downstairs in the morning, she was shortly followed by Tampion who, not finding her in the house, went to the nearest neighbours. Drawing a blank there, as he was walking home he spotted a woman's skirt floating in the pond about 60 yards from the house. Running to the pool he found his wife and dragged her from the water; despite 'every means being used to restore animation' poor Mrs Smith was no more.

8 NOVEMBER

1818 *Inquest at Framlingham.* In the days when many folk kept a loaded shotgun in the corner of the kitchen to bag edible wildlife and kill vermin from the window, it was not unknown for accidents to happen. On the previous morning, a Sunday, Mrs Mary Smith had been in the kitchen when her son Jasper (9) had picked up the gun. While carrying it across the room to the window it had gone off and mortally wounded Mrs Smith. Neighbours and the doctor were soon on the scene but poor Mary Smith had bled to death.

9 NOVEMBER

Bridewells and Prisons visited by Prison Reformer John Howard
Sudbury Gaol and Bridewell was only visited twice, in 1776 and 1779. A day room, complete with a fireplace, for debtors was recorded, along with two little rooms (measuring 7ft by 5ft) for them to lodge in. A room for 'men-criminals' was also noted as being replete with fireplace and loom; a similar arrangement existed for the women. A courtyard was noted as was the water supply not being accessible to prisoners.

10 NOVEMBER

1744 Final preparations were made for the local derby boxing match, to be fought at the Great Castle, Framlingham, the following day. John Smith, the Suffolk champion, had invited John Slack, the Norfolk champion, to meet at the ancient fortification to do pugilistic combat for the sum of 40 guineas. Hundreds came from miles around but in only a few rounds Smith was downed by the 'Norfolk Dumpling'.

11 NOVEMBER

WOVEN IN PURE SILK BY T. STEVENS, COVENTRY.

THE LATE

FRED. ARCHER.

1886 The interment took place of champion jockey Fred Archer (29) at Newmarket Cemetery. Archer was and remains a racing legend: among the classic races he won are six St Legers, five Derbys and four Oaks. Out of the 8,004 races run, he won 2,748. A champion jockey every year from 1874 until his untimely death in 1886, he was truly at the top of his craft. Tragically, all was not well with Fred Archer. Not only had he seen an infant son die in 1884, but his beloved wife died

12 NOVEMBER

(National Horse Racing Museum, Newmarket)

after complications during the birth of their daughter in the same year. Beset with family tragedy, Archer fought a progressively harder fight to maintain his weight, relying increasingly on a strong purgative known as Archer's Mixture. Coupled with the usual malicious gossip from some jealous of those at the top of their craft, it all proved too much for Fred and he took his life at his home in Newmarket, with a pistol originally given to him by a trainer to scare burglars. At the inquest, such was the interest in his death the coroner instructed a member of the jury to take the pistol and 'never let it see light of day' and so it remained until the National Horseracing Museum opened at Newmarket, where it may be seen with other Archer memorabilia today.

13 NOVEMBER   **1913**   *Girl in taxi adventure.* Young servant girl Maude Reeve (19) of Blaxhall, went to London in search of work. Over a period of a few months she was engaged in an eclectic selection of positions, remaining in them for only a short while and quitting each on an apparent whim. Eventually approaching Frederick Pitts, a Kennington taxi driver, outside Liverpool Street station she asked if he knew the way to Ipswich. Pitts said he knew the way and agreed a fare of 50s. On the way Maude said she wanted to be dropped at the Great White Horse Hotel near Ipswich. Arriving at the hotel, and arranging a return journey she went in to get a drink and the money. She simply asked Fred Hall, the Head Boots at the hotel, where the back door was and went out of it! Proceeding to Popplewell's cycle shop on Woodbridge Road, she hired a bicycle for 6d and rode off with no intention of coming back. These offences may seem minor today but in the genteel world of 1913 they were simply outrageous and made more so because they were committed by a young woman! A police alert was given for her apprehension and the press had a field day when she was captured a few days later at Tunstall by Inspector Norman.

At her trial it transpired she had obtained bicycles elsewhere, and had been in lodgings, paying nothing in either case but no proceedings had ever been instigated against her. Magistrates considered the matter and sentenced her to two months' imprisonment.

14 NOVEMBER   **1636**   A newsletter entitled 'Newes from Ipswich' began to be circulated. This tract made a general attack upon bishops for suppressing weekday lectures and sermons on Sunday afternoons, and for silencing puritanical ministers. It also appealed to the king against the 'persecuting prelates', with especial attention paid to Bishop Wren of Norwich. The leaflet, written by William Prynne under the pseudonym of Matthew White, saw to it that Prynne would receive the venom of his persecuting prelates. Brought before the Star Chamber in London, he was sentenced to lose the stumps of his ears, to be branded S.L. (seditious libeller) on both cheeks, to forfeit £5,000 and then be imprisoned for life.

NEVVES
FROM
IPSWICH:

Diſcovering certaine late deteſtable practices of ſome
dominiering Lordly Prelates, to undermine the
eſtabliſhed Doctrine and Diſcipline of our Church,
extirpate all Orthodox ſincere Preachers and prea-
ching of Gods Word, uſher in Popery,
Superſtition and Idolatry.

*Woe be unto the Paſtors that deſtroy and ſcatter the ſheep of my Flocke, ſaith the
Lord.* Ierem.23.1.

Firſt printed at Ipſwich, and now reprinted for *T. Bates*. 1641.

1685 Mary Boyce (20) died unmarried at Walsham le Willows. Some say she
died of a broken heart, but what is certain is that a fair young maid passing
without marrying in the nineteenth century was both unusual and tragic. In
Walsham church a 'maidens' garland' or crant was erected in her memory
and may be seen to this day under the clerestory windows. Suspended on a
wire loop from a horizontal iron rod, it is made of wood, on one side bearing
a skull and crossbones with the name of Mary Boyce underneath while on

the other side the date of 'Ye 15 NOVE-EMBER 1685' is recorded. It was a tradition that upon the anniversary of Mary's death, the memorial was decorated by parishioners with a wreath of flowers.

16 NOVEMBER   **1934** National and local newspapers and magazines were full of the story of sensational confidence trickster 'Major Crane' (real name David Percy Caplice), heir to the 'Wenhaston Millions'. Major L.T. Crane KM, CBE, appeared in Southwold in 1933.

Immaculately dressed and ingratiating himself into all the good circles of the town he began to take a few special friends into his confidence. He revealed that he and the Crown were joint claimants to what became known as the 'Wenhaston Millions'. The problem was he was being financially crippled by the legal wrangles to get the money. He even defrauded shrewd businessmen of thousands of pounds, who were led to believe a handsome share of the money would be theirs once the matter was concluded by the courts. Crane swore these trusting gentlefolk not to breathe a word of the matter to others, binding them to their promise by getting them to sign the Official Secrets Act. He was exposed when attempting to arrange his marriage to Mrs Duke, the housekeeper of one of his backers at Blythburgh. Mrs Duke needed a divorce and it was the influential Major who procured one for her. The Revd Pryke of Southwold saw through the forged documents immediately and alerted the police who already had suspicions about 'Major Crane'. Crane made a break for it, fled to Newhaven and left his clothes on the beach, as if he had committed suicide. Nobody believed this desperate ruse and 'Crane's' face was plastered over news-stands and under headlines. Hoping to 'disappear' in London, he hired a pony and cart, bought a stock of vegetables with his remaining money and began a grocery round at Hackney. It was there, in St Thomas's Road, that plain-clothes detectives arrested him. Brought back to Ipswich he stood trial for his frauds. The 'millions' were merely a figment of Caplice's deceitful imagination and the life of 'Major Crane' a tissue of increasingly bigger lies. Caplice was sentenced to four years' penal servitude.

17 NOVEMBER   **1893** The report of the inquest into the death of the paupers at Eye workhouse was published. In this truly tragic case, an elderly couple named Elijah and Ann Warnes, aged 90 and 85 respectively, were living at

Worlingworth in squalid conditions (in a house where even the walls did not align) and suffering from senile decay. After much persuasion and assurances of better care from the district relieving officer they were removed to the workhouse. The problem was that the relieving officer did not personally oversee the move. The cart arrived to take them on the appointed day, and it was bitterly cold. Orders were orders and the elderly couple were carried into the cart and the three-hour journey was made. Harry P. Riches, Master of the Eye Workhouse, stated that when they arrived they had not been properly covered up. When he saw them, Mr Warnes had on an overcoat and the couple were lying (on top of a bed of straw) on two cotton rugs, the end of which had been thrown over them. Dirty and freezing cold, they were sent directly to the infirmary. Elijah Warne died a few days later and was soon followed by his wife. At both of their inquests the cause of death was given as 'senile decay' (poor Anne was especially ill, having suffered hypostatic congestion of the lungs and an old intercapsular fracture of the neck of the right femur) but with strong reprimand from jury and coroner that death was hastened by their removal.

1894   A daring burglary took place at Alston & Moirs, on the Butter Market, Ipswich. The work was said to be 'undoubtedly the act of a professional burglar, a complete set of housebreaking tools left behind'. He had entered from the thoroughfare, climbing an iron gate, and forced a window. His progress was barred by a strongly locked door; he climbed back and returned with a jemmy. Picking the lock of the door to the shop, he gained entrance and a wholesale raid was enacted which gained the burglar a haul of about £100. Before leaving, the burglar changed his clothes and left behind what he had been wearing. The pepper-and-salt coat, waistcoat and brown overcoat with velvet collar had a stocking sewn in to hide the jemmy and 'loops and pockets about the clothes clearly intended for the reception of the favourite implements of the profession'. He also left behind a pencil with the initials P.H., a cheap bowler hat, trousers with frayed-out bottoms and 'soiled underclothing'. Despite all these clues there were no real police forensics or even fingerprinting; it appears this burglar was never caught, nor was any of the loot ever recovered.

18 NOVEMBER

1909   The report of a terrible accident resulting in the death of Albert Arthur Smith (41), labourer at the Grey Friars Works, Ipswich. Smith was attending to the chilled roller turnery when his right arm was caught and torn off by the drive belt. Death was practically instantaneous: the deceased had been revolved round the pulley which was making 160–180 revolutions per minute.

19 NOVEMBER

870AD   *The martyrdom of St Edmund at Hoxne.* Local folklore tells of how King Edmund, having evaded capture by the rampaging Danes, was revealed to a newlywed couple crossing Goldbrook Bridge by the reflection of his golden spurs glinting in the water. His hiding place betrayed, Edmund was

20 NOVEMBER

Statue of St Edmund
in the cloisters at
Bury St Edmunds.

King Edward the
Martyr Memorial,
Hoxne.

captured by the Danes, secured to an oak tree, scourged with whips and finally put to death by a volley of arrows, after which they beheaded him. His head was immediately snatched up by a wolf, taken to a secret spot and guarded until it could be reunited with Edmund's body and given a Christian burial. When Edmund's kinsmen came for the body, the wolf was seen guarding the head between its forepaws. Moved a safe distance away to Sutton the head and body were buried and a small wooden chapel was erected over the spot. At this tiny chapel miracles began to happen: sight was restored to the blind and speech to the dumb. The body was found to be incorruptible and the head had become reunited with the body! Edmund's body was removed thirty-three years after his death to Boedericsworth. From this humble settlement and shrine grew one of the most important religious houses and towns of Suffolk – Bury St Edmunds. The oak upon which Edmund was executed was venerated for generations until it split and collapsed in August 1843. Revealed by this split was an old arrowhead thought to have been contemporary with the martyrdom of Edmund. This remarkable find was noted in the address of Sir Arthur Harvey to the members of the Archaeological Institute in 1854. Shortly after the collapse of the tree a stone monument was erected on the site and may still be seen today. The split trunk and branches of the ancient oak were left near where they fell until it gradually rotted away or fell prey to souvenir hunters. The other legacy of Edmund in Hoxne is Goldbrook Bridge which is still believed to carry a curse, so newlywed couples often go on a diversion of several miles to avoid it on their wedding day.

The remnants of the Martyr's Oak at Hoxne, *c.* 1903.

1882 *Ticket-of-leave man.* Thomas James (38), who had been convicted of manslaughter at Winchester Assizes in March 1875, was handed down ten years' penal servitude and sent to Pentonville Prison in London. Liberated on licence of becoming a 'ticket-of-leave man' he was transferred from the Metropolitan Police District to Ipswich for a fresh start in November 1882.

27 NOVEMBER

The criminal record of Thomas James. (*Suffolk Constabulary Archives*)

Suffolk beliefs and omens that warn of the approach of the Angel of Death

Fires and candles afford presages of death. A candle can predict a winding sheet for a corpse if, after it has gathered, a strip of wax or tallow, instead of being absorbed into the general tallow, remains upright and unmelted by the flame, and is noted to curl away from it – it is a presage of death to the person in whose direction it points. If a hollow oblong cinder is spat out of the fire, it is a sign of a death coming to the family.

22 NOVEMBER

1901 Reports appeared of Colonel Samuel Franklin Cody, wild-west showman (not to be confused with Buffalo Bill) and pioneer aviator conducting flying experiments with his 'Viva Kite' at Bury St Edmunds. His flying device consisted of four large box kites, all of which were attached to a rope, from which the pilot was suspended in a wicker chair. Cody made two ascents, the last taking him up an estimated 800ft. The wind changed, causing the kite to career out of

23 NOVEMBER

Colonel S.F. Cody and one of his flying machines.

control, and the supporting line snapped, sending our brave aviator plummeting to earth. Fortunately his fall was broken by a leafless tree near the barracks and he lived to fly another day with his main injuries being rope burns to his hands. Flight was to be his death, however; he was killed in a flying accident on 7 August 1913, and was buried with full honours and thousands lining the route of the cortège to the military cemetery at Thorn Hill.

LINES
COMPOSED ON THE LIFE AND DEATH OF
EBENEZER TYE,
Who was Murdered at Halesworth, on the 25th November, 1862.

In Halesworth town, that very day
The people were in such a way;
Poor Tye was lost, could not be found,
So they did search the place around.

Some thought that he was kill'd, and put
In th' ozier ground, or in a moat;
With lights did many look about,
But could not find the poor man out.

Until at ten o'clock at night,
His body then was brought to light;
As Mister Lucas was passing by,
He saw the body of poor Tye.

It in the water there did lay,
And like a helpless lump of clay,
It had been there for hours, no doubt,
Before it was indeed found out.

The news soon o'er the town was spread
That poor Tye was found quite dead;
Well, this was his unhappy fate,
It much confusion did create.

An excellent character he bore,
By all the rich as well as poor;
Murdered he was, no doubt, by one
Who as a shock man was known.

His name is Ducker, the people say,
Who took the poor man's life away.
Hanging is too good for such;
Law cannot punish him too much.

The Coroner o'er his body went,
And Jurymen were quite content
That he was murdered by some one
Who this fatal deed had done.

Ducker then was brought to view,—
The Coroner and the Jury too;
He then did all the truth deny
About poor Ebenezer Tye.

But the same was all in vain;
In prison he must now remain.
In Ipswich Gaol, he there must dwell,
Until the Law his case fulfil.

The Judge will then his case decide;
The Hangman will a rope provide;
Then on the Gallows he must swing,
Because he did such cursed thing.

He would have laid it to a sweep,
Who was in bed, no doubt, asleep;
For this one thing he ought to die;
This no one living can deny.

He is a shocking man, no doubt;
His sins will surely find him out.

Let Ducker's equals warning take,
And their dreadful sins forsake.

They will not fear policemen, then,
If they walk and act like men;
Policemen will not trouble you,
But will like you better too.

Sergeant Taylor found the clothes
That did the murderer's dress compose;
He also took the body in,
And Ducker that did commit the sin.

Two hundred years indeed have flown
Since a murder there was known;
This the people do deplore,
And hope such will not be no more.

What would our country do, I pray,
Were not policemen in the way?
Why, we should not live at peace,
But crime would every day increase.

Policemen, then, encouragement take,
Your duty do, for conscience' sake.
Alas! poor Tye is now no more;
He died at the age of twenty-four.

By a murderer he was driven,
From earth, we hope, to dwell in Heaven.
May God his parents now sustain,
Who still in Woodbridge do remain.

May He support them by His power,
In this very trying hour.
His last remains were borne away,
To dwell within a house of clay;

To its last home, beneath the ground,
Until the Judge's awful sound;
Then all the dead, both small and great,
Must stand before the judgement-seat.

Murderers, then, in vain may call,
For rocks and hills on them to fall;
They did reject the God of love,
And shall not dwell with him above.

Much respect for Tye was shown,
By the tradesmen in the town;
Shutters were up in different places,
And tears did fall from many faces.

Policemen shewed him great respect;
All things were done for him correct.
The bell did toll an awful sound
While he was passing to the ground.

They bid his last remains good-bye—
Their much esteem'd, EBENEZER TYE.

Sold by the Author, WILLIAM DELF, Gardener, Ingate Street, Beccles.

(Suffolk Constabulary Archives)

1862   The murder took place of PC Ebenezer Tye (24) at Halesworth. PC Tye
was a good copper; in the eighteen months he had been in the East Suffolk
Police Force he had already been commended for 'extraordinary courage after
being severely treated by some parties who he had apprehended for larceny'.
Ordered to observe a John Ducker (63), a hay trusser of Clarke's Yard,
Chediston Street, Halesworth, 'from 5 o'clock until breakfast time', Tye took
post in full uniform and galoshes 'for the purposes of deadening tread'. Tye was
last seen alive at 5.40 a.m. about 50 yards from Ducker's house. When he did
not turn up for duty that evening there were fears for his safety, and police
officers were dispatched to Ducker's house to investigate. Ducker denied all
knowledge but Tye's body, lying face-down in a sewer-laden stream at the rear
of Chediston Street where a number of privies emptied, was found by PCs Lucas
and Cattermole at 10 p.m. Ducker was immediately questioned again about his
black eyes, an injury to his wrist and a gash to his forehead. Ducker tried to
blame it on accidents while chopping wood, using a hay knife and a comb.
Searching Ducker's house, police officers discovered clothes saturated in water
and mud with stream weeds in the lining. When the stream was dragged,
Ducker's cap was recovered from the water. Piecing together witness statements,
it appears PC Tye had observed Ducker stealing hay and wood from a
neighbour. Challenging him, Tye probably found himself outclassed. Despite
being considerably older, Ducker was a strong man who had been known as a
'notorious wrestler' in his day. In a conversation with Ben Warne, the chimney-
sweep, Ducker had even confided after being asked if he had seen the
policeman, 'I'll be damned if I haven't done for him.' The post-mortem, carried
out in a nearby stable by Dr Frederick Haward, revealed considerable bruising
but the cause of death was suffocation by drowning. Whether Tye had been
forcibly held under water or left unconscious to drown was never fully
ascertained but either way it was murder. The jury at the assizes agreed and
Ducker was executed at Ipswich on 14 April 1863. He has the dubious
distinction of being the last man to be hanged in public in Suffolk (*see* 14 April).

1876   *A singular case of fright.* A hawker who gave his name as John Brown of
Worcester was very drunk and being taunted by boys in the marketplace at
Bury St Edmunds. He caught hold of the nearest boy, a lad named Prigg,
threw him down and began to kick him. The boy got up and ran away, and
Brown gave chase. Seizing the boy, he pushed him into the doorway of a Mrs
Clements and pulled his hair. Mrs Clements came to the door and attempted
to intercede. Brown pushed her away and poured out a tirade of abusive
language at her. She was so terrified she was struck with paralysis for days
after. At the court proceedings Mr Hinnell, the surgeon, stated he had little
hope of her recovery. Brown was given seven days for the assault on the boy
and fourteen for the attack on Mrs Clements.

1586   *The Great Fire of Beccles.* Beccles has endured major fires in 1586, 1662,
1667 and 1669. The first fire destroyed more than eighty houses, and property
to the value of £20,000. A broadsheet produced at the time concluded:

Each stately Towre with mightie walls up prope
Each leftie Roofe which golden wealth hath raised
All flickering wealth which flies in firmest hope
All glittering hew fought and highly praised
I see by sodaine ruine of Beckles towne
Is but a blast of mighty love do frowne.

27 NOVEMBER **1876** Reports of the petty sessions at Harleston related the case of Elizabeth King, charwoman of Bungay, charged with stealing sixpence and several articles of clothing, the property of Mrs Peek. It appeared she had stolen the money and taken the clothes for a night out in Bungay. Electing to be dealt with by the bench, she was sentenced to three months' hard labour.

28 NOVEMBER **1924** Frederick Southgate (52) was executed at Ipswich Gaol for the murder of his wife. Southgate had recently split up with his wife. A court order was obtained to keep him away but he still insisted on attempting to enter the marital home on John de Boise Hill in Ardleigh near Colchester. An argument developed between Southgate and his wife; she turned to run away, and made a few steps, but Southgate was too quick with his knife and plunged it into her back. A neighbour, Johnnie Bruce (16) bravely intervened, Southgate fled on his bicycle, and all poor Johnnie could do was cradle Bet Southgate in his arms as she died. Southgate fled to Colchester and handed himself into the mental asylum. Identified by the summons in his pocket he was soon in custody. Despite working hard to maintain the insanity plea and lack of memory Southgate was proved at Chelmsford Assizes to be sane and culpable for the murder of his wife and kept his appointment with the hangman at Ipswich.

29 NOVEMBER **1826** James Reeve was a well-known rabbit dealer around the Woodbridge area in the winter season. On one dark night Reeve was returning with his pony-and-cart laden with rabbits when there was a fatal jolt; one wheel of the cart went by the side of the arch and turned it over a few rods from the Cherry Tree at Bromeswell. When the accident was discovered the pony was almost dead in its hafts and poor old James Reeve was found quite dead, covered from head to foot with his cart's burden – smothered by a load of rabbits.

30 NOVEMBER **1888** At Suffolk Winter Assizes, Jonathan Marsh (23), John Morphey (30) and Samuel Pryke (28), all labourers, were charged with night poaching with violence at about 3 a.m. on 23 November at Baylham. The prisoners were each sentenced to nine months with hard labour.

December

This monument commemorates the twelve Protestant Martyrs burnt at the stake
in Bury St Edmunds during the reign of 'Bloody Mary'. Situated in the Great Churchyard,
it is pictured here in 1910.

1 DECEMBER **1885** The peaceful bustling of the streets at Long Melford on polling day was shattered by the arrival of about 400 men in procession from Glemsford, determined not to be dissuaded or told how to vote by their masters. Marching with banners bearing the title 'Union is Strength' and led by a band, any hope of a peaceful conclusion to the march was lost through incompetence, bureaucracy and misinterpretation on all sides at the polling station. The marchers became unruly and stones were thrown, smashing a number of windows. Within half-an-hour Captain Bence, a local magistrate, began swearing in special constables to supplement the extra thirty officers who had been drafted in for the march. This was misheard by marchers, who thought he was reading the Riot Act, and open violence erupted. Many police and local people received injuries from the flying bricks; many of the marchers were already fired by alcohol. Turning into Hall Street, the mob stormed the Crown pub, totally ransacked it, and drank any alcohol they could lay their hands on. At 5 p.m. the Riot Act was read (for the last time in Suffolk) and troops of the Suffolk Regiment which had been telegraphed earlier arrived 15 minutes later with an additional ten policemen. The police regrouped and marched up the town with truncheons drawn, followed by Captain Scudamore and his men of the Suffolks with fixed bayonets behind. This had the desired effect, and the rioters dispersed. Many arrests were made and fines issued at the magistrates' court. The ringleaders appeared at High Court but were each acquitted when the court agreed the authorities were equally to blame for the events through their ill-considered and inadequate voting arrangements.

Long Melford, *c.* 1905. It is hard to imagine that a violent riot took place here in December 1885.

1875   In the days when whole villages turned out for wedding celebrations, this day should have been greeted by many in the glow and hangover haze of the morning after the night before, but the people of Debenham and Stonham woke up on this day reaching for mourning black and kept their shutters drawn. Popular local congregational school teacher and choirmistress Miss Caroline Butcher had been joined in holy matrimony to Mr Freeman by the Revd C. Cornish at Debenham church. While she was being was being transported to the reception that was to be held at her eldest brother's home at Stonham, young Caroline complained of pains in her side. Her feelings were put down to nerves and the festivities continued. Tragically the pains persisted and intensified to such an extent the party was stopped; her new husband left with his sisters to summon the doctor but before they could return 'she peacefully departed this life'.

1899   A shocking tragedy occurred as an Ipswich labourer named Thwaites killed both his wife and himself, and almost killed a man named Hudson. Mrs Thwaites had left her husband and had gone to keep house for Hudson. Thwaites rolled up at Hudson's house, gained entry and locked the door behind him. When the police were summoned, following reports of gunshots from the property, they had to break down the door. Hudson was discovered with gunshot wounds. Thwaites was discovered on the floor with a revolver in one hand and a knife in the other. His wife was found stabbed and shot by his side.

1875   *Destitution in Ipswich*. A tragic case emerged this day before the borough coroner H.M. Jackaman Esq. at the Black Horse Inn, St Mary Elms, on the body of a young man named John Chisnall. The son of a well-liked postman in the Capel and Bentley area, the deceased had been apprenticed and proved himself very able in the trade of painter and glazier. The inquest revealed: 'he fell into the habit of drinking and became utterly demoralised and broken in health'. Losing work because of his drinking, he descended into living 'a wretched life', earning stray pence for odd jobs. He took a squalid room in a tenement paying 1s a week. He had no bed but slept on canvas with old bags to cover him. His landlord returned from his early morning drinking session at the Elephant and Castle, and found Chisnall with his clothes soaked and stinking as if he had dived into the river. It had been a bitterly cold morning and the tenement was little warmer than outside. Chisnall could take no more and 'slowly, peacefully and insignificantly' dropped into stupor and faded away.

1905   The report was published on the inquest into the death of Thomas Smith, an Ipswich shoemaker. Smith was a widower with four children, two of whom were in St John's Home. A poor but sober and proud man, he simply could not make ends meet on his meagre wages. With certain legal proceedings hanging over him, he confided to friends he would 'do away with himself'. Mr Charles Brooks was walking along the towing path near the river when he saw a cap hanging on the palings and a shoemaker's hammer in the grass. The police were contacted and the murky river dragged. The body of

Smith was recovered, with his hands tied behind him and a severe wound inflicted on his forehead. Dr Hetherington, Borough Police Surgeon, was convinced the man could have fastened his hands behind him, a measure probably resorted to if he failed to knock himself unconscious into the water. A verdict of 'suicide during temporary insanity' was returned.

6 DECEMBER **1905** Two workmen employed by the Ipswich Corporation in the preparation of land for building in a meadow about 50 yards from the Hadleigh Road unearthed the skeleton of a woman in a state of excellent preservation. The body was found about 2ft below the surface, buried in a recumbent position with the knees drawn up. The police were informed and when examined by local experts she was thought to have been about 5ft 7in tall and around 45 years of age. The report notes: 'a peculiar fact is that on one side of an otherwise perfect head is a small oblong shaped hole, which cuts clean into the skull'. Another body, a male skeleton, was recovered a short distance away a few days later. Both were thought to be of considerable antiquity.

7 DECEMBER **1899** Aldeburgh lifeboat was returning from routine service in high seas when she was struck by a heavy curling breaker which fell on the boat broadside-on and capsized her. Most of her crew managed to scramble out but six remained trapped under the upturned hull. Despite prompt efforts to turn the boat over or smash an entry, the boat drifted to shore when all life was found extinct and six brave local lifeboatmen were put in early graves.

8 DECEMBER **1929** With criminal records as long as many local people's memories George Whistlecraft, known locally as 'Joe', and his brothers were notorious poachers and familiar faces to local police and petty sessions. With so much covert activity by night over so many years, something had eventually to go horribly wrong. Local folk were used to the stories of 'thump-ups' and threats between the Whistlecrafts and gamekeepers but there was real shock when the local community heard that Charles Cornwell had been shot and killed while pursuing men he was certain were Joe and Ernest Whistlecraft in Stubbing Wood, Botesdale. Mike Scott, who had been with Cornwell during the incident, summoned the local police and Inspector Brown arrested the brothers at their cottage. As the case developed, statements and evidence were collected, Ernest was released and Joe stood alone on a charge of murder. At a trial that attracted wide interest from across Suffolk and beyond, Whistlecraft pleaded 'not guilty'. The case revolved around the rifle used: the police had taken two guns from the Whistlecraft house but apparently the wrong one was presented in court. Whistlecraft was found 'not guilty' and walked free from the court (*see also* 5 November).

9 DECEMBER ### Suffolk Old Dame's Leechcraft
To prevent swelling from a thorn, circle the middle finger of the right hand quietly pronouncing:

Christ was to a Virgin Born,
And crowned with a crown of thorns;
He did neither swell or rebel,
And I hope this never will.

At the end, after the words have been thrice repeated, touch it every time with the tip of your finger, and with God's blessing you will have no more trouble.

1906 At the turn of the twentieth century Monday police courts and Borough Benches in the bigger towns and ports would often be full of those who had over-indulged the previous weekend. Here are three cases from Lowestoft which appeared on this date. John Goodrum, fish hawker, who did not appear was fined 10s for being drunk. PC Warner said the defendant had been fighting and was using obscene language. Daniel Lincoln, who had four previous convictions, had been found drunk and disorderly in Commercial Road after ejection from the Commercial Stores and was fined 15s. Finally a 'pungent vagrant' named John Child had been caught drunk and begging for alms in Clapham Road. After pointing out that his police cell had been 'one of the most comfortable I have been in for a long time', Child said he had tramped from Longton and would tramp back if they let him go. He was sent on his way.

10 December

1778 A thump-up between the press gang and a party of men at the Green Man, Ipswich. A Mr T. Nicholls, master of the Ram Inn, who interfered, was so badly beaten up that he died the next day. A charge of wilful murder against two midshipmen and fifteen of the press gang failed at the Court of the King's Bench at Westminister the following year.

11 December

A thump-up with the press gang.

12 December — **Bridewells and Gaols visited by Prison Reformer John Howard**

The County and Town Gaol, Ipswich, was visited on six separate occasions between 1774 and 1782 when Rowland Baker and, later, John Ripshaw were gaolers. There was only one courtyard. For debtors, there was a kitchen, or day-room one of which was made into a free ward. Felons had a day room

and a 'strong night room' for the male prisoners complete with 'beds well contrived for cleanliness and health'. Each prisoner had a crib-bed about 10–12in high with strong feet and low sides, the head raised a few inches. Howard observed, 'These are easily moved when the ward is to be washed. The county allows to each crib a straw bed, and a blanket.' The women did not have a separate day-room – their ward or night room had no fireplace. Howard noted that 'One of the two drinking rooms is called the garnish room.' The two rooms for the sick were 'not distinct from the rest' and there was no bath. Debtors were seen to be occupied weaving on hand frames. Howard reported 'good garters [and also that the prisoners made] . . . purses, nets and laces which they sell at the front gate'. Howard remarked, 'I found this close prison clean, though full of prisoners.' The courtyard was found inoffensive because the water from the pump was conveyed through sewers. On one of Howard's visits, he commented on the 'neat chapel newly built'; in the centre of the ceiling was an aperture covered by a small turret which kept the room airy and pleasant. Howard noted the Revd

County Hall and Gaol, Ipswich *c.* 1909.

Brome, the chaplain, 'does not content himself merely with regular and punctual performance of his stated duty; he is a friend to the prisoners on all occasions'. With the assizes held (at that time) at Bury, the gaoler was provided with £6 6s for each prisoner's transport thither. It is also recorded that every debtor received 1¼lb of beef for broth, a penny loaf and a pint of ale courtesy of a legacy of Mr Pemberton's charity. From another legacy the town supplied five chaldron of coals yearly.

The Gaoler's Fees for the County of *Suffolk* agreed upon 29 of March 1676 by the Justices of the Peace underwritten.

	£.	S.	D.
Inprimis for every person committed in court - - - -	0	1	8
Item for every person committed out of court - - -	0	3	4
Item for every person committed upon warrant or process - - -	0	3	4
Item for every person committed upon execution - - - -	0	6	8
Item to the turnkey - - - - - -	0	1	0
Item for every person upon his acquittal for felony - - -	0	6	8
Item for every person committed upon outlawry - - - -	0	10	0
Item for every prisoner lodging in the gaoler's bed for every night taking no diet in the house - - - - - -	0	0	6
Taking diet - - - - - -	0	0	4
If he find his own bed and take diet - - - -	0	0	3
If he take no diet - - - - -	0	0	4
Item for every prisoner that is not a felon that will go into the ward and lye there for every night - - - - -	0	0	2
Item if two lye in one bed and take diet in the house for both - - -	0	0	6
If they take no diet - - - - -	0	0	8
For the two best chambers in the house as they can agree.			

Henry Felton	*Anth*. *Gawdy*	*Tho*. *Edgar*
Rob. *Brake*	*Tho*. *Bacon*	*Charles Milton*
Tho Smith	*Tho*. *Bade*	
		Ex per Ro. Clarke V. C. P. Com.

1906 An inquest was held into the death of Emma Eliza Catchpole, a domestic servant in the employ of Mrs Mann of 'Sunnyside' at the little village of Geldeston on the Norfolk–Suffolk border. Emma had left her previous employer after being 'let down in a promise of marriage by a young man'. In the following months he had apparently written to her only once after a chance meeting, and her depression only deepened. Emma had asked Mrs Mann if she could leave her employ on Tuesday 11 December, and although notice was short, Mrs Mann consented. Mrs Mann's nephew, Frank Hall, who also lived in the house, stated that at 7 p.m. he had seen Emma as she cleared the tea things away. She was heard moving around in her quarters but did not respond to a bell at 8 p.m. Frank stepped into the kitchen to find Emma hanging from a piece of cord fastened to a nail in the scullery ceiling; the chair she had stood on lay kicked away against the fireplace. Dr Crowfoot was summoned from Beccles but when he arrived he found Emma 'quite dead'. The jury pronounced the kindest verdict they could under the circumstances: 'suicide whilst temporarily insane'. **13 December**

Suffolk beliefs and omens that warn of the approach of the Angel of Death **14 December**
On this day it was traditional to mark where mistletoe grows, for Christmas decorations, but under no circumstances should any be brought in until Christmas Eve. It was also prudent to examine sources for holly and ivy, for if yew was brought into the house among the evergreens used to dress it for Christmas, there would be a death in the family before the year was out.

15 DECEMBER

Suffolk Old Dame's Leechcraft

To cure bleeding from the nose, wear a skein of scarlet silk round the neck, tied with nine knots down the front. If the patient is a male, the silk should be put on and the knots tied by a female and vice versa.

———•—•———

To cure bleeding from wounds repeat these words three times, desiring the blessing of God:

> Stand fast; lie as Christ did
> When he was cruicified upon the cross;
> Blood, remain up in the veins,
> As Christ's did in all his pains.

16 DECEMBER **1894** Poor John Dale (20), a Lowestoft smacksman, lay dying in Lowestoft Hospital. A couple of days before, he had attended the fair at the Old Market Place, Lowestoft. Paying his penny for a ride on the swing-boats, he rose from his seat while the swing was in full motion to change places with a companion. Missing his hold, he was dashed to the ground with a fall of about 16 or 17ft. Smashing his arm and rendered unconscious, he died on 17 December. The inquest recorded accidental death and exonerated the proprietors of the boats of all blame.

17 DECEMBER **1887** Charles Beavis was heard to use obscene language on Haverhill High Street by PC Ransom. The policeman had cautioned Beavis about the swearing, whereupon Beavis repeated the language and walked away. At the Haverhill Petty Sessions the bench was 'determined to put a stop to the use of such vile language' and so Beavis was sentenced to fourteen days without hard labour.

18 DECEMBER **1887** Samuel Taylor, a gamekeeper in the employ of Mr Barrell, was night-watching the woods at Redgrave with his brother Arthur when shots were heard in Carpenter's Grove. Through the falling snowflakes they observed two men exiting the wood, so Samuel and his brother ran after them. The brother caught one, while Samuel Taylor was knocked to the ground and struck by a stick. A struggle ensued and both called for help but the poachers' mate got there first and, with a blow to the back of the head, struck Samuel to the ground where he was kicked and rendered unconscious. Attended by doctors, Samuel Taylor ended up being laid up for three weeks before full recovery. On the night of the incident Inspector Grimwood of Botesdale had been summoned to the scene and made good progress. In the light snow the tracks of one of the assailants were traceable over the four or five miles to the door of his house! The man in question was Philip Wilby. Confronted by the inspector after being tracked to his door, he could not deny being present at the incident. Arrested and taken to the police station, Wilby was examined and found to have several cuts to his head and blood on his collar; when asked to account for these he replied, 'I'll wait till I sees how the case goes.'

At the Winter Assizes, Wilby was charged with poaching with 'divers persons unknown to the number of three or more'. Wilby was found guilty and sentenced to two months' imprisonment with hard labour.

19 DECEMBER — **1748** The parish register of Monks Eleigh records on this day that Alice Green, the wife of a poor local labourer, was swum after 'malicious and evil people having raised report of her being a witch'.

20 DECEMBER — **1795** The Henstead blacksmith Thomas Pleasance died on this day. His charming epitaph reads thus:

> My Sledge and hammer lies reclined,
> My Bellows, too have lost their wind,
> My Fire extinct, my Forge decay'd,
> And in the Dust my Vice is laid.
> My Coals are spent, my Iron's gone,
> My Nails are drove, my work is done.

21 DECEMBER — **1866** In the days when illegitimate birth was common but frowned upon, the stigma of being a single mother proved to be too much for some. On this day Lizzie Gentry came to lodge at the house of Elisha Deal at Lavenham. No doubt removed from her home in Essex for her confinement, the poor young woman's emotions gradually dipped further and further into the abyss. Having been let down by a cad who promised marriage, once she had given birth she was inconsolable in her depression. Just days after the birth, Lizzie stuffed the baby's mouth with her handkerchief and cut its throat. The nurse who was sleeping in the room was aroused by the commotion and summoned the master of the house, who saw young Lizzie had also cut her own throat. Mr Barkway, the surgeon, was sent for, but there was nothing to be done. At the inquest, a verdict of murder was given on the death of the child and suicide while in a state of temporary insanity for tragic Lizzie.

22 DECEMBER — **1893** The case was reported of John Lord, who was arrested for stealing a coat belonging to Mr Soar at Messrs Meadow's and Jewesson's Office. Placed in a police cell, Lord hung himself by attaching his neckerchief to a bar of the window. At the inquest a verdict of *felo-de-se* was returned.

23 DECEMBER — *c. 1750* *A few last-minute Christmas gifts recorded in Suffolk from the mid-eighteenth century.* How about a book entitled *Round about our coal fire; or Christmas Entertainments*, described as 'containing Christmas Gambols, Tropes, Figures with abundance of Fiddle-faddle stuff such as stories of Fairies, Ghosts, Hobgoblins, Witches, Bull-Beggars, Raw-Heads and Bloody Bones, Merry Plays etc for the diversion of Company in a cold winter evening'; or what about *Christmas Treat or Gay Companion*, a new collection of Merry Stories, or even *A Christmas Box for Gay Gallants and Good Companions*, containing 'Diverting stories, Choice Jokes, Dextrous tricks, Pleasant poems, Rare Riddles and jovial songs'?

24 December **1892** *The Barnby train disaster.* At about 7 p.m. on Christmas Eve, around 5 miles from Lowestoft, one of the most horrific train accidents in the history of Suffolk occurred. On this single rail line, about a quarter-of-a-mile from the Beccles signal-box, was a loop used to allow trains to pass each other. A dense fog had enveloped this area. The Lowestoft train had reached Barnby and was about to run onto the loop line to make way for the approaching Beccles train when the two locomotives smashed with such impact that the Lowestoft engine was 'forced through concussion' into the middle of the third-class carriage. 'By the fitful gleam of lanterns and flickering glare from a large bonfire which had been made out of wreckage close by the Ambulance Corps proceeded with their mournful duty'. The local papers carried lists of all the casualties and detailed their injuries but only three were found dead at the scene. Mr Read, the fireman on the Beccles train, had had his head 'battered in a shocking manner'. As he was laid out on the freezing grass, the handkerchief laid over his face was 'almost frosted to his features'. Beside him was soon laid the body of Mr Lake, the guard on the Beccles train, who had been thrown to the floor by the force of the impact and crushed by shattered woodwork. Despite some horrific injuries, only one passenger died at the scene. Mr Mallett, found alive but 'horribly crushed', died in the hands of those who released him.

25 December **1823** A copy of Christmas verses presented to the inhabitants of Bungay by their humble servants, the late watchmen (forerunner of the police force), John Pye and John Tye:

One of the 'Charlies' of the Watch.

Your pardon, Gentles, while we thus implore,
In strains not less *awakening* than of yore,
Those smiles we deem our best reward to catch,
And for those which we've long been on the *Watch*:
Well pleased that we recompence obtain,
Which we have ta'en so many steps to obtain,
Think of the perils of our *calling past*,
The chilling coldness of the midnight past,
The beating rain, the swiftly driving snow,
The various ills that we must undergo,
Who roam, the glow-worms of the human *race*,
The living Jack o'Lanthorns of the place.

'Tis said by some, perchance to mock our toil,
That we are prone to '*waste the midnight oil*',
And that a task thus ide to pursue,
Would be an 'idle waste of money too',
How hard, that we the *dark* designs should rue
Of those who'd fain make light of all we do,
But such the fate oft doth merit greet,
And which now fairly drives us off our beat,
Thus it appears from this our dismal plight,
That some love *darkness* rather than the *light*.

Henceforth let riot and disorder reign,
With all the ills that follow in their train,
Let Toms and Jerrys unmolested brawl,
(No Charlies have they now to floor withal,)
And 'rogues and vagabonds' infest the Town,
For cheaper 'tis to save than crack a crown . . .

To you kind sirs, we next our tribute pay:
May smiles and sunshine greet you on your way,
If married, calm and peaceful be your lives;
If single, may you forthwith get your wives
Thus whether Male or Female, Old or Young,
Or Wed or Single, be this burden sung:
Long may you live to hear, and we to call
A Happy Christmas and New Year to all.

1647   A few heads, not just sore through over-imbibing the day before, were suffered this day in Bury St Edmunds. The Puritan Parliament had abolished Christmas and the Bury apprentices did not like it! About 150 of their number met near the market cross and, whipped into a furious mob bent on direct action, set about urging shop-owners to close for Christmas, smashing any who dared to argue. Only when troops had been summoned and entered the streets of the town did the rioters consider ceasing their rampage.

26 DECEMBER

The ancient village armoury in the Priest's Room, Mendlesham Church.

27 December

Strange and Horrible Tales of Suffolk

Mother Munnings of Hartis was tried before Lord Chief Justice Holt at Bury in 1694. Many things were deposed concerning her spoiling of work and hurting cattle, and that several persons upon their deathbeds had complained she killed them. She threatened her landlord that his nose should lie upward in the churchyard before the next Saturday and before that day he died. She was charged with having an imp like a polecat. A person swore that one night passing her cottage he saw her take two imps, one black and another white, out of her basket. She was acquitted.

28 December

1881   Joseph Watson (21), a navvy, murdered Mary Anne Squirrell (22) at Ipswich. Mary was living with her parents (Mr and Mrs Bumpstead) after she had separated from her husband. Returning home one afternoon Mrs Bumpstead found Watson asleep on the couch with her daughter sat on a stool beside him. A row broke out; Mrs Bumpstead wanted Watson out of the house and he left with Mary. Joe and Mary spent the rest of the day in two pubs, Mary spending most of her time trying to dissuade the drunk Watson from 'doing something on his mind'. At 11 p.m. they were seen by the docks, and witnesses recalled hearing a woman's voice call out 'Don't be so cruel Joe; oh don't!', and a man replying, 'I'll be —— if I don't drown you.' A splash was heard. Alice Tricker stated she saw Watson throw his arm round Mary's waist, raise one of the quay chains with his other hand and then both stooped and rested on the quay for a moment, the woman on the man, then they rolled into the water. Cries were then heard from the water from each to save the other. Poor Mary drowned and Joe Watson was brought to trial at the assizes. The jury found him guilty of murder but with a recommendation for mercy. Sentenced to death, Watson's date with the hangman was cancelled and commuted to penal servitude. Having served his term Watson was released on 10 July 1892

29 December

Suffolk Old Dame's Leechcraft

A plan for discovering and punishing a witch. If you have good reason to believe you are bewitched, get a frying pan, pull hair out of your head, and lay it on the pan, cut one of your fingers and let some of your blood fall on the hair. Then hold the pan over the fire until the blood begins to boil and bubble. You may then expect the witch to come and knock at your door three times wanting to borrow something, and hoping to make you talk. But you must hold your peace. If you utter a word, you will be more bewitched: if you refuse to speak, you will so work upon the witch's blood as to cause her such pain she will beg your forgiveness; and then you will be set free.

30 December

Last Rites

Victorians loved statistics and the compilation of records. One great exponent of all the information at his disposal was John Glyde junior, who, in his book *Suffolk in the Nineteenth Century*, used facts and figures to analyse and moralise about the social conditions of Suffolk. One such series of statistics

The charnel house and gates in the Great Churchyard, Bury St Edmunds.

reveal the number of deaths from occasional outbreaks of what medical authorities referred to as Zymotic diseases in the county of Suffolk. During 1840–2 and 1848–9, 153 persons died of smallpox, 330 of measles, 1,097 of scarlatina, 510 of whooping cough, 490 of diarrhoea, 129 of cholera, 1,692 of typhus and 292 of influenza.

New Year's Eve

Folklore in Walsham le Willows stated that a witch was knocked down and fatally injured by a coach which failed to stop. With her dying breath she cursed the coachman. It is said that the coachman was now doomed to make the journey complete with his spectral coach on the same road from Walsham to Stanton. It is said all who see it are supposed to drop down dead, or 'know death' within a few days of the sighting.

31 December

A Calendar of Suffolk Executions, 1824–1924

John Chenery, Benjamin Howlett, Thomas Wright, Robert Bradman (all executed for burglary) 21 April 1824 (Largest simultaneous execution in Suffolk since the seventeenth century)*

John Mann (highway robbery) 20 August 1825*

William Corder (The Red Barn Murder) 25 April 1828*

George Partridge (murder) 13 April 1829*

William Cattermole (arson) and Thomas Hubbard (burglary) 25 April 1829

Samuel Wright (unnatural offence) 17 April 1830

Ambrose Flack (murder) 25 July 1831

William Turtchell (burglary) 15 August 1832*

Benjamin Edwards (arson) and James Stroulger (arson) 18 August 1832 (The last double execution in Suffolk)

William Jolly (arson) 17 August 1833

Edward Chalker (murder) 30 March 1835

George Pulham (arson) 8 April 1835*

Mary Shemming (murder) 11 January 1845

William Howell (murder) 25 January 1845

Catherine Foster (murder) 17 April 1847

George Cant (murder) 22 April 1851* (Last execution at Bury)

Mary Ann Cage (murder) 19 August 1851 (Last woman executed in Suffolk)

William Flack (murder) 17 August 1853

Ebenezer Cherrington (murder) 17 August 1858

John Ducker (murder) 14 April 1863 (Last public execution in Suffolk)

Henry Bedingfield (murder) 3 December 1879

Thomas Lyons Day (murder) 13 November 1883

George Sanders (murder) 16 February 1886

George Nunn (murder) 21 November 1899

Arthur Garrod (murder) 20 June 1911

Frederick William Storey (murder) 16 June 1920

Frederick Southgate (murder) 27 November 1924 (Last execution in Suffolk)

* Denotes execution at Bury St Edmunds.
All other above executions were performed outside or within Ipswich Gaol.

After 1924 Suffolk felons under sentence of death were executed at Norwich Prison until the abolition of capital punishment. These were:

Walter Smith (for murder on Felixstowe Docks) 8 March 1938

Arthur Heys (for murder at Ellough) 13 March 1945

Acknowledgements

It has been proved yet again that you can meet some of the nicest people while doing some of the grimmest research. I extend specific thanks to the following, without whose generous assistance or contributions this book would not have been so enriched – or so grim! Paul Hydar, Les Jacobs and Neil Longdin from Suffolk Constabulary; the generous advice of Chris Mycock at Moyse's Hall Museum; David Jones at Ipswich Museum; Dr Stephen Cherry; the Revd Andrew Thomas; the Church of St Michael the Archangel at Beccles; Mrs G. Tilley from the United Reformed Church at Bury St Edmunds; James Nice; Geoffrey Scott; Peter Newman; the late Syd Dernley; the very helpful staff at Suffolk Record Offices at Bury St Edmunds, Ipswich and Lowestoft; my old friends at Norfolk Local Studies Library in Norwich.

In my travels researching this book it has been a pleasure to meet many very helpful and interesting people along the way. There are too many to mention all by name, but an especial 'thank you' is extended to the good people I encountered at Woodbridge Museum and Dunwich Museum; the National Horse Racing Museum at Newmarket; the Swan Inn at Hoxne; Stiffkey Lamp Shop and in the churches at Southwold, Orford, Walsham le Willows, Redgrave and Nacton.

Usual respects are paid to Tony Smith from Shutters and Terry Burchell for their photographic wonders. Every attempt has been made to contact the owners of copyright for images used in this book. If any omission has been made it is not deliberate and no offence was intended.

Finally, I thank my family for their love and support for this temperamental author, especially my son Lawrence, who has accompanied me on several expeditions to explore the unusual side of history in Suffolk.

*Note: All pictures are from the author's collection, unless otherwise credited.
All the modern photographs of monuments, gravestones and historic sites were
taken by the author on his travels across Suffolk over the last ten years.*

Places to Visit

Moyse's Hall Museum
Cornhill
Bury St Edmunds
IP33 1DX
01284 724821

Ipswich Museum
High Street
Ipswich
IP1 3QH
01473 213761

Dunwich Museum
St James Street
Dunwich
IP17 3EA
01728 648796

Southwold Museum
9–11 Victoria Street
Southwold
IP18 6HZ
01502 722437

National Horse Racing Museum
99 High Street
Newmarket
CB8 8JL
01638 667333

The figure of Justice on the domed roof of Bungay Butter Cross.